W9-CQK-354

UNDERSTANDING THE TRAGEDY

Terror
Over America

Virtually all Scripture references are quoted from the King James translation of the Holy Bible.

Terror Over America

Copyright ©2001 by Midnight Call Ministries
West Columbia, South Carolina 29170
Published by The Olive Press, a division of Midnight Call Ministries -
P.O. Box 280008, Columbia, SC 29228 U.S.A.

Copy typist:	Lynn Jeffcoat, Kathy Roland
Copy Editor:	Angie Peters, Susanna Cancassi
Proofreaders:	Angie Peters, Susanna Cancassi, Micah Froese
Layout/Design:	Michelle Kim
Text Layout:	Ryan Guerra
Lithography:	Simon Froese
Cover Design:	Michelle Kim

Library of Congress Cataloging-in-Publication Data

Froese, Arno
      Terror Over America
      ISBN #0-937422-54-1

      1. Prophecy

All rights reserved. No portion of this book may be reproduced in any form without the written permission of the publisher.

Printed in the United States of America

This book is dedicated to the
Church of Jesus Christ worldwide.

It is intended to contribute toward a better
understanding of God's counsel to men
based on the Scripture.

The author does not benefit through
royalties from the proceeds
of the sale of this book. All received funds
are reinvested for the furtherance
of the Gospel.

CONTENTS

5

INTRODUCTION

"…shall there be evil in a city and the Lord hath not done it?" (Amos 3:6).

The moment I witnessed the horrendous catastrophe that befell the World Trade Center and the Pentagon and realized that this was an unprecedented act of terror against civilians, I decided to analyze this world-shaking event from a biblical perspective. As Bible believers, we know that God has everything in His control. But we also realize that Satan is the god of this world and the prince of darkness, and he does his work of destruction in the children of disobedience.

To begin with, I must say that this book is not anti-Muslim. We have no intention whatsoever to point an accusing finger at any nation, whether Afghanistan, Iraq, Libya, Iran or any other. The purpose of this book is to reveal what God says about these matters through prophecy, which He will fulfill even though He may use diabolically inspired people on earth in doing so.

Never in modern history have we witnessed such an outpouring of sympathy for America as after this tragedy.

9

Virtually all Arab countries sent their condolences and the civilized world expressed its compassion for the victims and their families in a most moving manner. This response clearly was not part of a political game of politeness, but a genuine expression of the sorrow and pain the people of the whole world shared with America.

We must realize that this event is something that brings us more than just one step closer to a united world. Virtually all political leaders the world over, military experts and those whose task is to assure safety and security for their citizens, were united in their statements: We need an international understanding and full cooperation to hunt down those who are responsible for the atrocity and to paralyze, if not totally annihilate, all terrorist organizations in the world!

Deliberately we have not listed the many details that were reported in the media during September 11 and the days following because that is the task of the very capable news media, particularly those in the United States of America. Our motive for writing this book is to enhance the spiritual vision of believers, to place this event in its proper perspective in God's plan of salvation, and to show Satan's opposition to that plan through the use of destruction and death.

The many wars and conflicts, primarily of a religious nature, throughout Europe caused many nationals to pack their bags and sail across the sea to a continent called America, North and South. The U.S.A. in particular has become a beacon of justice, individual rights and freedom for many people and nations. The United States' contribution towards the development of global democracy has been phenomenal.

When we follow history, we see that after great wars or catastrophes, something new usually has been established. Note that the two world wars, particularly World War II, caused the birth of the United Nations, which has become the most significant organization for most nations in the world.

The pages of this book will also reveal several reasons for the great conflict between Christianity and Islam on the one hand and the tiny country in between, Israel, on the other hand. How the act of terror against the United States fits into this development and what it means to Christians is the central theme of this book.

The bottom line of this message, however, is to cause the reader to run toward the one place of security: Jesus Christ.

Chapter 1

THE ACT OF TERROR

From the impact on the north tower at 8:45 to the collapse of that tower, 100 minutes transpired. These 100 minutes represent the greatest terror in America's history as well as the most horrendous act of terrorism the world has seen.

For the first time in history, the process of such an event was shown globally so that the potential eyewitnesses via satellite television could reach into the billions.

In our local newspaper, *The State*, dated September 12, we read:

> "Terrorists plunge hijacked planes into the World Trade Center towers in New York and the Pentagon. New Yorkers react with disbelief: 'This is the most horrifying thing I've ever experienced.' The toll at the Pentagon is 'extensive.' Some lawmakers say U.S. intelligence network has atrophied."

Engineering News Record reported in its September 17, 2001 issue on page 12:

> "I was trying to clear the area of sheetrock…and just

as I was filling the dumpster, the whole building shook, it swayed back and forth," recalls Trykowski. "I thought at first it was an earthquake." He and 70-odd workers hit the stairwell as water pipes broke and panic flared. As he went down, a group of firemen were going up, never to be seen again.

London-based *Financial Times*, September 12, 2001, page 1:

"After two hijacked passenger aircraft destroyed the World Trade Center in New York, and another hit the Pentagon in Washington, the White House was evacuated and Air Force fighters were scrambled to try to counter airliners that were hijacked and used as serial bombs."

In *Time* magazine's special edition for September 11, 2001, James Kelly, Managing Editor, introduced the magazine with these words:

"I got up a little earlier than usual last Tuesday. My day, perhaps like yours, was shaping up to be pretty busy, so I wanted to get a head start. A little before 8 a.m., I kissed my wife and son goodbye and headed to Time's offices in midtown Manhattan. By 8:30, I was at my desk, answering e-mails. Shortly before 9 a.m., Steve Koepp, the deputy managing editor, called on his cell phone from downtown. Walking his son to school, he could see that a plane had crashed into the north tower of the World Trade Center."

U.S. News & World Report's issue dated September 24, 2001, began its special report on page 10 with these words:

"The terrorists flew on devil's wings in a horrifying moment, singular in history. They changed the course of a presidency, a nation, and, quite likely, the world."

An insurance correspondent for the *Financial Times* made this statement in the September 12, 2001 issue on page 2:

> "The huge loss of life in the attacks in the US could turn out to be the most costly disaster in the history of the insurance industry."
>
> "It is safe to assume claims will be in billions," said Robert Hartwig, chief economist for the Insurance Information Institute.
>
> Analysts said the cost to life assurers and insurance companies through employers' liability and workers' compensation schemes was likely to be even greater than the claims for property and aircraft.
>
> The losses would be covered, Mr. Hartwig said, as acts of terrorism were covered under insurance policies in the US.
>
> AIG, the world's biggest insurer by market capitalization, will be heavily exposed to the disaster — not least because its Manhattan headquarters on Pine Street are close to the World Trade Center.
>
> Munich Re, the world's largest reinsurer, said claims stemming from the attacks could be considerable but they would not threaten the company's financial stability.
>
> Shares in Munich Re, Swiss Re and Allianz were among the hardest hit. Swiss Re said it was too early to say what the group's exposure would be.
>
> One London dealer said: "This is not a markdown. People are actually selling the insurers, and it's particularly heavy for the reinsurers who take on a lot of the risks for disaster insurance."

The effect of this act of terrorism was not limited to New York and Washington, but it reached across the ocean to affect the entire world.

Chapter 2

GLOBAL REACTION
TO TERROR

When I entered the local bank at approximately 9:08 on September 11, 2001, the teller told me the news: Two planes had hit the World Trade Center. When she said "two," my mind immediately raced to the conclusion of a terrorist attack. As I drove back home, the chaos became evident as I listened to a newscaster on the radio interviewing an eyewitness overcome with emotion. It had been more than just some small planes rented by terrorists who were planning to commit suicide. This involved two large passenger airplanes. By the time I got back to the office, there was no other news being broadcast but the attack on the World Trade Center. Seeing the clear pictures transmitted over satellite TV, I recognized the crippling effect of the attack upon these two towers. "That will take many long months to repair," I casually observed to my family. Never in my wildest dreams would I have thought that these gigantic buildings would collapse.

Suddenly another news flash broke into the coverage we were watching: At 9:48 a.m., an American Airlines Boeing 757, Flight 77, carrying 58 passengers and 6 crew members, crashed into the Pentagon.

Forty-nine minutes later, the south tower of the World Trade Center collapsed and at 10:35 it disintegrated into dust and ashes.

The shock was overwhelming. I was speechless and perplexed. Not long after that, the first calls began to come in from family, friends and co-workers overseas. They all had seen the same thing; they all had heard the same news and everyone seemed to echo the same refrain: this had happened unexpectedly, and was an unbelievable nightmare come true.

Statesmen the world over were quick to send condolences to the President of the United States and the American people. From all continents and virtually all countries, the world expressed anger and shock over the tragedy that had come suddenly upon America.

A Moment Of Silence

Financial Times, under the headline, "Assault On America," wrote in the September 13, 2001 issue on page 2:

> Financial markets were open for business outside the US — but business did not seem to be a top priority. Bankers and traders across the world were either mourning colleagues lost in the destruction of the World Trade Center or checking to see if they were safe.
>
> All the main European markets, including the London, Frankfurt and Paris stock markets, observed a minute's silence at 12:45 GMT, as a mark of respect. All the US markets in New York and Chicago were closed, and the securities and Exchange Commission was due to meet the heads of the Wall Street firms and the exchanges to decide whether they should reopen.
>
> "People almost feel guilty to want to trade for profit in

circumstances like these," said a senior banker in London. "We are not encouraging people to speculate [in the markets]." The mood instead was one of solidarity, even among usually intense competitors.

Deutsche Bank offered to transact the foreign exchange dealings of Citigroup, its arch-rival in that part of the market.

European Union finance ministers, the ECB, other EU central banks and the European Commission pledged "all necessary measures to ensure the proper functioning of markets and the stability of the financial system." They added: "We stand ready to provide, in close cooperation with the US, all support which might be needed. The central banks in the EU have declared that they will continue to provide liquidity for the smooth operation of payments and settlements systems."

One senior British banker said banks had practiced their disaster-recovery procedures extensively but that this would be the first time "they have been used in anger."

One immediate result of this tragedy was instantly evident: unity.

Media Unity

The media, at its best, holds a mirror up to what can be seen. And US television producers offered a grieving nation reflected images of its own wounds. The strain, the thought and courage that went into these recordings are remarkable. The achievements of journalists are not akin to the heroism of rescue workers, but they did recover for the rest of us a sense of what we have lost.

Not every image broadcast has been spectacular, not every report accurate, not every minute effectively edited. The overriding fact of this collective enterprise is that it had a common public-service purpose — no advertising to interrupt or capitalize on the tragedy.

As ABC's Peter Jennings said in the early Wednesday hours, the networks had even shared their footage, laying aside the fierce competition that would characterize an ordinary day.

NBC gained early access to the devastation through a few right-place, right-time producers, who gathered riveting footage that kept recording long past what safety would dictate.

The doctors were given the chance to explain who each victim was, without permitting names or faces to be revealed. Exploitation was blessedly absent.

The power of these images should be wielded only delicately. Interviewing politicians has proved another touchy power play. The appearance of defense secretary Donald Rumsfeld on several networks demonstrated the importance of face time for national leaders. His boldness seemed even to give a provocative interviewer such as CBS's Dan Rather pause.

Television has done its best when it preached the least and showed the most. Hardly any serious journalist embarks on a story without this aim in mind, but contemplating terror brings its own distortions. Reporters making sense of the new world have so far done much to deserve our most profound concentration.

Mayor Rudy Guiliani has been perhaps the frankest and most reassuring voice. His deflection of body-count questions — "more than we can bear" — have helped to guide the coverage back to the sublime.

–Financial Times, 9/15–16,01, P.6

Political Unity

Statements made by world leaders revealed an unprecedented unity. *The State* newspaper, September 12, 2001, page A10 said this:

European governments expressed solidarity with the United States as a democratic ally under attack Tuesday night.

There was quiet discussion among European officials Tuesday night about how they could help the United States respond to Tuesday's attacks. Russian president, Vladimir Putin, also expressed support for retaliation.

Criticism of President Bush and his foreign policy, particularly his plans for missile defense, was silenced. Countries moved quickly to defend U.S. embassies and institutions on their soil.

Expressions of solidarity and condolence poured forth.

French President Jacques Chirac cut short a visit to Britain to return to Paris. He said he felt "immense emotion" over these "monstrous bombings," and that the French "are entirely with the American people."

France put its security forces on alert. Army and policy personnel were on the roads, at borders and at airports.

At the airports, armored cars were stationed along the runways and there was more baggage screening.

British prime minister, Tony Blair, expressed his disgust, saying, "This mass terrorism is the new evil in our world today." He called an emergency meeting of his security officials in the face of what a Defense Ministry official called "a pretty serious crisis."

Putin, a key member of the U.N. Security Council, promised support for retaliation against those responsible in a telegram to Bush.

"Such an inhuman act must not go unpunished," Putin wrote. "The entire international community should unite in the struggle against terrorism."

In Germany, Chancellor Gerhard Schröder called the attacks "a declaration of war against the entire civilized world," and in a statement, he said he had assured Bush "of Germany's unlimited solidarity." He ordered German flags to fly at half-staff at all official buildings. A black flag was raised over Austria's parliament.

German foreign minister, Jaschka Fischer, wrote a letter of sympathy and solidarity to his American counterpart, Secretary of State Colin Powell, saying, "We are speechless and disgusted by the terrorist attack on New York and Washington."

A key foreign policy adviser, Karsten Voigt of the Social Democratic Party, said in an interview that all allied democracies stood with the United States.

"It shows we must stick together," he said.

"We hope the United States is learning that it does not stand alone. We in Germany stand on your side and will do everything to support you and help you in this common struggle against the evil in the world. This is a war against civilization, and we are with you."

Karl Kaiser, the director of the German Council on Foreign Relations and an adviser to Schröder, said that the openness of democratic societies has been "bought at the price of vulnerability, vulnerability so high that you can conduct a war inside democracies."

For the first time since the British burned down the White House in 1814 and the attack on Pearl Harbor in 1941, he said, "The Americans experience what Europeans have experienced: war on home territory."

Those responsible for the attacks will be identified, Kaiser said, "Then America will strike, and hopefully not alone."

The NATO secretary-general, Lord Robertson, said the attacks "constitute intolerable aggression against democracy and underline the need for the international community and the members of the alliance to unite their forces in fighting the scourge of terrorism."

Greece, criticized by Washington for its laxness in

fighting terrorism, also moved to protect U.S. institutions.

–By Steven Erlanger
The New York Times

How true are the statements of those world leaders who pledged support for the United States? As true as political opportunity presents itself.

Dozens of other significant reports make it crystal clear that one enemy still stands in the way for the world to unite into a true global family: Terrorism!

Chapter 3

SHADOWS OF PROPHECY

The Bible tells us that the leaders of the world in the end will *"…have one mind, and shall give their power and strength unto the beast"* (Revelation 17:13). This is a key thought we must keep in mind when analyzing this great tragedy and we must also realize that this is just one step in the process towards the fulfillment of Bible prophecy.

We have to understand that a new global world is being created. The whole world will live in peace and prosperity and even religiously the world will be so united that *"…all that dwell upon the earth shall worship him,"* meaning the Antichrist.

Such a goal can never be attained without deception, however. Even closely related democracies in the western world do not agree with one another on every occasion. To form a truly global unity, the world's largest populated country, Communist China, must also be fully integrated. Besides, the world of Islam, with 1.18 billion adherents, must be appeased and somehow made to compromise in order to become an equal member of the family of nations. This can only be done through deception.

Here we must recall that Satan, titled "the father of lies"

because there is no truth in him, is the originator of deception. Scripture reveals him as the god of this world who works in, through and with the children of disobedience to attain his goal.

The prophet Daniel speaks of the Antichrist in chapter 11:21–24a, *"And in his estate shall stand up a vile person, to whom they shall not give the honour of the kingdom: but he shall come in peaceably, and obtain the kingdom by flatteries. And with the arms of a flood shall they be overflown from before him, and shall be broken; yea, also the prince of the covenant. And after the league made with him he shall work deceitfully: for he shall come up, and shall become strong with a small people. He shall enter peaceably even upon the fattest places of the province...."* Three words must be highlighted:

1) peaceably
2) flatteries
3) deceitfully

The word *"peaceably"* is mentioned twice in these few sentences.

What does it mean? It simply shows us that the New World Order will not be established by the force of war but peaceably — through negotiations, signed treaties, and cooperation among the nations. That, incidentally, is exactly what every normal human being desires. No one wants a son, daughter, husband or wife to risk losing his or her life by going to war. We all choose the way of peace. Whether Jews or Christians, Muslims or Hindus, Buddhists or atheists, communists or capitalists, socialists or dictatorships, every person on the face of the earth wants peace — but each on his or her own terms, and that's where the problem comes in.

From a heavenly perspective, there is a different problem because war, disagreement and controversy are caused by one little word, "sin." For that reason we as Christians know with absolute assurance that no nation, no movement, no NATO, no European Union, and no United Nations will be able to produce a lasting peace.

Lasting Peace

Peace is not only the absence of conflict or war, but it is a gift of God. I'm speaking of the peace that passes all understanding. This peace can only be obtained through faith not in a system, but in a person, the Son of God, Jesus Christ of Nazareth. He paid in full the cost for all sin of mankind, which is the cause of war. When He poured out His blood on Calvary's cross and exclaimed, *"It is finished!"* the payment was made in full. Now every one who comes to Him in faith asking forgiveness for sins will receive it. The only peace we can be assured of is the one we can offer through the Gospel to anyone. But this is not a collective peace; it is individual. It is not based on a treaty, negotiation or compromise. It is not written with ink on paper, but it is sealed with the blood of the Son of God. He guarantees in John 14:27, *"Peace I leave with you, my peace I give unto you: not as the world giveth, give I unto you. Let not your heart be troubled, neither let it be afraid."*

The Antichrist

Who is the Antichrist? In short, he is the masterpiece

of Satan, a man according to the heart of man. We must take special notice of the words we already highlighted previously, *"peaceably" "flatteries"* and *"deceitfully."* In the same chapter, Daniel writes, *"…they shall speak lies at one table…"* (verse 27). We must understand the fundamental principles of political negotiation. No matter which nation, negotiations are always based on self-serving advantages. No politician ever argued for his opponent; no nation ever highlighted the good of another nation, particularly of an enemy nation poised for war. This attitude of "me, myself, and I" is precisely the spirit of the Antichrist.

Further, we read in verse 36, *"And the king shall do according to his will; and he shall exalt himself, and magnify himself above every god, and shall speak marvellous things against the God of gods, and shall prosper till the indignation be accomplished: for that is determined shall be done."* This is selfishness to the utmost: *"his will," "exalt himself," "magnify himself"*!

Not surprisingly, we are being taught in schools and colleges, and even in churches in these days, to increase our self-worth, and to do everything in our power to reinforce our self-esteem. But such philosophy is diametrically opposed to the Scripture. We are invited to follow Jesus. Who is He? Isaiah 53:3 gives the answer, *"He is despised and rejected of men; a man of sorrows, and acquainted with grief: and we hid as it were our faces from him; he was despised, and we esteemed him not."* Why did we not esteem Him? Because He humbled Himself, *"And being found in fashion as a man, he humbled himself, and became obedient unto death, even the death of the cross"* (Philippians 2:8).

These characteristics are contrary to those of modern man.

Preparation For The Future

Let us take another look at the Antichrist whom the Bible says will rule the world. The apostle John is the only one who uses the term "Antichrist," and he wrote that even at his time, there were *"many antichrists."* What does that mean? It simply means that the preparation for the kingdom of Antichrist on earth began during the times of Jesus.

We must also realize that Jesus offered the perfect kingdom of heaven to the people of Israel when He came. He proclaimed the same message John the Baptist had preached to the people, *"Repent ye for the kingdom of heaven is at hand"* (Matthew 3:2). But the people of Israel rejected this offer; subsequently, the kingdom was taken away from them. Israel was destroyed and the Jews were dispersed over all the nations of the world. That fact, however, does not change God's eternal prophetic Word because He will establish His kingdom on earth and He will make peace among the nations globally. He will fulfill Micah 4:3, *"And he shall judge among many people, and rebuke strong nations afar off; and they shall beat their swords into plowshares, and their spears into pruninghooks: nation shall not lift up a sword against nation, neither shall they learn war any more."*

In the meantime, however, the great deceiver, Satan,

whose title is also the great dragon, the old serpent, and the devil, who is the father of lies, fights desperately against the establishment of the kingdom of God on earth.

How does he do it? By deceiving all the people on earth to believe that man is capable to bring about peace based on his own strength.

The Birth Of Sin

We read of Satan's origin (called "Lucifer" in the KJV translation) in Isaiah 14:12–14, *"How art thou fallen from heaven, O Lucifer, son of the morning! how art thou cut down to the ground, which didst weaken the nations! For thou hast said in thine heart, I will ascend into heaven, I will exalt my throne above the stars of God: I will sit also upon the mount of the congregation, in the sides of the north: I will ascend above the heights of the clouds; I will be like the most High."*

This glorious *"son of the morning"* had a self-esteem problem: *"I will ascend" "I will exalt" "I will ascend" "I will be like the most High"* that's the beginning of sin. Lucifer's first success was to deceive the serpent, who in turn deceived Eve and Adam; thereby man, who was created in the image of God, became a servant of Satan.

Therefore, it stands to reason that servants of Satan, who is the great destroyer, a murderer from the beginning, cannot bring about peace. Subsequently, all negotiations and peace treaties proclaimed by politicians the world over cannot bring about lasting peace. But mankind, in general, believes that he is capable of producing such peace without the Prince of Peace. As a result, all the politicians of the world will continue to work feverishly towards that one goal: peace for mankind.

That is why Satan will succeed in bringing about an unprecedented unity among the world's population. We must point out that Satan is not the Antichrist, but the Antichrist is a person fully inspired by the devil.

Antichrist Receives Power

When we read in Revelation 13, we note that the first beast, the Antichrist, who comes out of the sea of people is apparently a powerless person, a poor fellow who has nothing on his own — no credentials, no army, no political system, and no power whatsoever. But then we read in verse 2: "...the dragon gave him his power, and his seat, and great authority." Verses 4 and 5 confirm: "And they worshipped the dragon which gave power unto the beast...there was given unto him a mouth speaking great things and blasphemies; and power was given unto him to continue forty and two months." Furthermore, we read in verse 7: "And it was given unto him to make war with the saints, and to overcome them: and power was given him over all kindreds, and tongues, and nations." We have carefully noted that the Antichrist, called the beast, who comes out of the sea receives everything from the dragon, which is identified in chapter 12:9 as "...the great dragon...that old serpent, called the Devil, and Satan...." So finally, Antichrist will have power "...over all kindreds and tongues and nations." What will be the result? "And all that dwell upon the earth shall worship him...."

When we analyze the tragedy of September 11, 2001, we must attempt to understand the big picture, the entire history of mankind. This terrible terrorist attack was not an isolated act of aggression and brutal murder, but it was part of a process Satan is using to unite the world into one people and to move them to the point at which they will look unto one person to be their absolute leader. That person will be the Antichrist.

Chapter 4

ATTACK ON AMERICA
IN LIGHT OF PROPHECY

"And his power shall be mighty, but not by his own power: and he shall destroy wonderfully, and shall prosper, and practise, and shall destroy the mighty and the holy people" (Daniel 8:24).

The great tragedy that has befallen America is unprecedented in her relatively young history. The agony, pain and suffering will not be over in a few months, but will continue indefinitely, especially for the family members and loved ones of those who have perished.

The devastation we saw on live television and heard described by eyewitnesses seemed like impressions from a science-fiction movie. Many said, "I can't believe it," or "I must be dreaming." Others said, "The reality has not set in; I can't grasp it." One eyewitness actually said, "I thought some Hollywood movie was being shot." But the tragedy was all too real. It wasn't a movie; it wasn't science fiction. It was a most brutal, inhuman and sadistic attack on the symbols of Americanism: The World Trade Center. It was an attack on modern civilization, on peace-loving people, on law, order and decency.

The attack on the Pentagon — a symbol of world

security—was executed to show the world that terrorism can defeat even the most powerful armed forces in the world.

The third target, which was missed, was to be either the White House or Capitol Hill, both globally recognized symbols of the strongest democracy in the world. Clearly, the terrorists carefully planned their strategy to show the civilized world its vulnerability.

Although America has lost thousands of lives during various wars throughout our history, we always have had a recognized and definable enemy. However, the attack on September 11, 2001 was different. The suicide terrorists were residing in the United States, and they used American aircrafts for their murderous act. They are all dead.

Those who planned and guided the attack do not have a country with a flag, a constitution or established borders. They have no legal ambassadors to other nations, nor do they have an industry that could be clearly identified or associated with their country. They have no written law except their own interpretation of Islam. And as early investigations reveal, they are scattered over the entire world, united only by their unbridled hate against all who are not Muslims, particularly residents of Israel and the United States. This indeed is an enemy the likes of which we have never confronted before.

This tragedy totally shocked all, including the military, the intelligence officials and the government. Although tens of thousands of people occupy themselves with the defense and security of the American people, they were all taken by surprise.

How To Understand The Evil

American citizens were shaken by the news. We mourn with those who are mourning and we weep with those who are weeping. The pride of America has been hurt deeply. Many are asking, "Is there an answer to such a tragedy?" "Will there be counter attacks, and on whom?" "How will the security officials have to act in the future?" "Is it possible at all to avoid such tragedies in the future?" These and many other questions are natural and we all are occupied with trying to find the answers.

In order to better understand this tragedy, we need to differentiate between the things that belong to the world and the things that belong to the Church of Jesus Christ.

We must seek to see the background and reasons for such a catastrophe. After all, the Bible says, *"…shall there be evil in a city and the Lord has not done it?"* Although the god of this world, the devil, rules the nations, he still is subject to the final authority, which comes from the God of creation, the God of Israel. Let us look at parallels in the Bible:

Pharaoh

Pharoah was the first destroyer of the nation of Israel when he commanded every young male child to be drowned in the Nile River. This was the work of the evil one, Satan, the destroyer. But God used this evil act to cause Moses to be brought into the family of Pharaoh and he ultimately became the savior of the children of Israel as he led them out from bondage into freedom.

Pharaoh, who intended to destroy the children of Israel

by water, was destroyed by water himself when he crossed the Reed (Red) Sea with his 600 chosen chariots.

Haman

Later in history, we are confronted with another enemy of the Jews: Haman, the Agagite. This diabolical man planned the annihilation of the Jewish people. As a symbol of his hatred, he intended to hang Mordecai, the Jew, on the 75-foot-high gallows he had built on his property. But the result is recorded for us in Esther 7:10: *"So they hanged Haman on the gallows that he had prepared for Mordecai."*

The Jews were not annihilated; in fact, the opposite took place: *"And in every province, and in every city, whithersoever the king's commandment and his decree came, the Jews had joy and gladness, a feast and a good day. And many of the people of the land became Jews; for the fear of the Jews fell upon them"* (Esther 8:17).

Hitler

In more recent history, we are introduced to another evil man, Adolf Hitler, ruler of Germany. He implemented "The Final Solution," his plan to destroy all the Jews on the face of the earth. He and his henchmen murdered over 6 million Jews during the Holocaust. The majority cremated in the gas ovens in concentration camps scattered throughout Europe. How did Hitler die? His body was doused with gasoline and burned beyond recognition.

The atrocities of the Holocaust and the turning away of

Jews by virtually all countries brought about the founding of the State of Israel on May 14, 1948.

World Unity

The events of September 11, 2001 made the call for world unity more evident than ever before. It seems as if suddenly, in a moment, all the world's leaders recognized that this horrendous terrorist attack was not an isolated assault on the United States, but one targeting the entire civilized world. Globally it was realized that the greatest enemy is terrorism.

Our modern world has progressed to the point that war between developed nations is virtually out of the question. It is unthinkable, if not outright impossible, for Canada to attack the United States, France to declare war against Spain, or Germany to invade Poland. These scenarios belong to the past. The nations of the world are so interdependent that nothing but great damage would come to any nation that would go to war against another.

Therefore, with reasonable assurance we can say that the western world lives in peace and security. Democracy rules the nations and is marching forward victoriously over planet Earth. However, not all nations of the world are fully integrated into the family of democratic nations. Developing nations in particular are under great pressure to follow in the footsteps of the successful nations.

Subsequently, world unity is an absolute must in order to fulfill Bible prophecy. Keep the words "world unity" in mind as you continue reading the pages of this book.

Chapter 5

SHADOWS OF ARMAGEDDON

O ne of my first overseas conversations after the event of September 11, 2001, was with Peter Malgo, President of Midnight Call International, headquartered in Switzerland. He mentioned his editorial for the October issue of *Mitternachtsruf* (Midnight Call) and e-mailed the copy to me. Here is the translation:

> *"And the kings of the earth, who have committed fornication and lived deliciously with her, shall bewail her, and lament for her, when they shall see the smoke of her burning, Standing afar off for the fear of her torment, saying, Alas, alas that great city Babylon, that mighty city! for in one hour is thy judgment come. And the merchants of the earth shall weep and mourn over her; for no man buyeth their merchandise any more...For in one hour so great riches is come to nought"* (Revelation 18:9–11,17).

An Israeli citizen said, "This is happening because of us; we must apologize."

September 11, 8:45 A.M., 2001: The world is shocked. A collection of several catastrophes with destructive force and intensity heretofore unimaginable has occurred. The precise timing of the individual terror acts within a short period of time clearly point to a perfectly organized plan behind which a satanic-inspired power stands.

The immediate reaction of joy among the Palestinian population in East Jerusalem, Samaria and Judea, over the successful attack against the United States of America did not help to reinforce any credibility of Yasser Arafat's public expression of regret and sympathy he addressed to the U.S.A. for its loss of life and material.

It seems that the great enemy of Israel increasingly shows his hatred, even outside the Jewish state, against those who in any way, shape or form cultivate friendly relations with the state of Israel.

The border between terror and war has been broken. Germany's chancellor Gerhard Schröder made this statement: "This is a declaration of war against the entire civilized world."

The most widely recognized symbols of capitalism, the two towers of the World Trade Center, were reduced to dust and ashes. Stock exchanges the world over registered great losses. Material values were reduced to nothing in a short time. Thousands of people died. The first reaction from eyewitnesses on the street: "The world will never be the same."

No doubt, world history has begun a new chapter. The shocking pictures of a smoked and dust-filled New York skyline seem as if they come straight from headlines in the newspaper reporting on Revelation 18. Such a scenario was unthinkable just a short while ago, but this event has made Revelation 18 a possibility. September 11, 2001 cast a shadow of the apocalyptic description the Bible contains. It seems unimaginable, but it is real. What is striking is the fact that it only took about one hour for the symbol of world's riches to collapse in ashes and dust.

The biblical proportions described in Revelation 18 do not directly apply to this tragic event because this was only a shadow of things to come. But such an unprecedented event should cause each of us to think about what is to come. Twice we read the words "one hour" in the book of Revelation. The two towers of world economy went up in smoke in "one hour." The entire world, paralyzed and in shock, helplessly watched the destruction.

Feverishly, politicians and the news media attempted to analyze the event, find the reason and identify the perpetrators. America's president clearly indicated that the source of this evil originated in a foreign country. Many compared this to the 1941 attack of the Japanese at Pearl Harbor. But very few public figures consider these events in light of the future. There is much talk, debate and expressions of frustration but all seem to detour from the God of the Bible. No one seems to ask about the background of this tragic event. As believers, we know that this did occur with the permission of the Almighty.

What must we as Christians say? Our concerned co-workers in Korea called and pointed to Luke 21:28, *"...when these things begin to come to pass, then look up, and lift up your heads; for your redemption draweth nigh."* We pray that these tragic and shocking events may bring us closer to Him who holds the future: *"He which testifieth these things saith, Surely I come quickly. Amen. Even so, come, Lord Jesus"* (Revelation 22:20).

Chapter 6

EXAMPLE: ISRAEL

" *N* *ow all these things happened unto them for ensamples: and they are written for our admonition, upon whom the ends of the world are come"* (1st Corinthians 10:11).

The catastrophic events of September 11, 2001 in New York and the Pentagon were not the result of one man or of an isolated group that thinks it has the capability of destroying America and taking over the world.

Behind each action, particularly behind events of such gigantic and global proportion, stands the power of darkness, the god of this world, who has blinded the eyes of the people so they may not recognize the truth and become free from the clutches of Satan.

The Bible says that we should not be ignorant of Satan's devices. If Christians left the analysis of this event to the world's news media and our political leaders and we would be guilty of not identifying the deeper causes of the tragedy.

When Jesus came to His people, they did not receive Him. He said, *"…if thou hadst known, even thou, at least in this thy day, the things which belong unto thy peace! but now they are hid from thine eyes…because thou knewest not the time of thy visitation"* (Luke 19:42,44). The people of Israel were expected to read, study and believe the Scriptures which testified of Jesus. The Jews were expected to understand but they didn't; they failed to heed the prophetic Word.

How does all this relate to the terrorist bombing in the United States? First of all, the United States' entire gigantic intelligence-gathering information complex did not think that such an attack was possible. No airport had the slightest idea that a number of the passengers who boarded those four planes were suicidal terrorists. It's unreasonable to assume that anyone should have foreseen such an event.

However, because the Bible specifically says that Israel has been given to us as an example, should we not have looked at Israel and learned from them?

The American intelligence was well aware that suicide terrorists have been operating throughout Israel, killing and maiming as many Jewish people as possible. Wouldn't it be reasonable to assume that some of those leaders might have considered what would happen if a group of these Muslim fundamentalist suicide terrorists were to come to the United States? After all, the American flag has been burned openly throughout the Arab world. Extreme factions of Muslim fundamentalists have publicly and loudly proclaimed that America is "the great Satan" and needs to be destroyed. But quite apparently, nothing had been done. Not only the United States, but also the entire western world must admit that their intelligence operations and subsequent preparations failed.

We plainly see that there is a distinct difference between Israel and all the nations of the world. Just look at modern history. In January of 1949, Israel shot down five British fighters over the Sinai who failed to properly identify themselves. Several other planes were also shot down as they approached Israeli airspace.

Unity At All Cost

American President George W. Bush made this statement from the Oval Office that Tuesday night: "…our friends and allies join with all those who want peace and security in the world, and we stand together to win the war against terrorism."

From these few words uttered by political leaders and from thousands of statements by news anchors and other members of the media, it becomes crystal clear that the whole world must unite.

Who in his right mind would oppose an international committee that is responsible for security against terrorists? I assume virtually no one except the terrorists. Thus we see a foreshadow of the fulfillment of the words, *"…these have one mind,"* in progress; in this case it's for the good. Cooperation will not be achieved because of some conspiracy or force of evil, but because it will be the right thing to do. Our security, our future and the well-being of our children and grandchildren is at stake.

Security…But How?

Again we must look at what the Scriptures say. The apostle Paul, inspired by the Holy Spirit, wrote of the Jews in 1st Corinthians 10:6: *"Now these things were our examples...."* I have already mentioned that Israel is our modern example. She has been threatened by suicide terrorists for decades; we should have learned. As far as security is concerned, we can indeed learn from Israel.

I have visited Israel many times since 1974. From that very early date on, I have not been crazy about the excessive security precautions taken by Israeli agents. For example, when arriving at New York City's John F. Kennedy Airport, one immediately notices that the entrance of the El Al Airline facilities look somewhat different than all others. Large concrete and steel pillars separate the street from the entrance. Outside the facility, a trained eye quickly notices two or three camouflaged security agents carefully watching arriving passengers. Another security agent opens the door to let passengers in, and before they enter the ticket counter area, each is interviewed (actually interrogated) by a trained security agent who asks a barrage of questions: What is your name? Why are you going to Israel? Who paid for your trip? Are you going with a group? What does the group do? Do you know any people traveling with you in this group? Do you have friends in Israel? Have you ever been there? What was his or her address in Israel? Where does your family live? Such simple questions are well crafted. Passengers who have anything to hide find it most difficult to keep their cool.

After a long question-and-answer session, the security agent asks to be excused for a minute, walks over to another agent and converses with him in Hebrew while the traveler watches. Then other agents take the passenger's ticket and passport and begin the interview process all over again.

Some of our fellow travelers have become so upset about the extent of the interrogation they have been ready to walk out the door, although they had nothing to hide.

We all know Israel has its reasons for taking these security measures. We also know that Israel is the prime target of the world's terrorists. Yet until this point, only one of its aircraft has been hijacked.

When our tour group landed in Frankfurt to change planes on the way to Israel, we were segregated into a different departure lounge. There every bit of our luggage was thoroughly searched, leaving virtually no possibility that we could board the plane with anything not known to the security agent.

Those investigative measures offer one way of making sure our airlines are safe; however, there is one problem. How can a security system screen off passengers who have nothing to hide—no gun, no explosives and no knives? The answer is that it simply cannot be done.

The September 11 catastrophe has brought into view a totally new side of terrorism: suicide terrorists. It stands to reason that if a terrorist organization wishes to hijack a plane, it can comply 100% with all the security requirements. All it has to do is send a half-dozen or more suicide terrorists who are highly trained in man-to-man combat to overpower any crew and take control of the aircraft.

Before the attack on America, no security system took

this possibility into consideration. But today it has become the most deadly one. Think about it for a minute. On any flight to any destination, a group of terrorists can board, take control of the plane, and execute their diabolical intentions.

Can Terrorists Be Recognized?

Now we come closer to the key words we employ in this book: *"...these have one mind."* We have already discussed the fact that all nations of the world must stand together in their fight against terrorism. That is, they must become of one mind. But even if that can be achieved, there is one question that has not been answered: "How do you differentiate between a "normal" passenger and one who has the intention of bringing the plane down?"

We just discussed how Israel has done this successfully for many years. One of Israel's advantages is that virtually all of its security agents were born and educated in Israel. They know how to distinguish between an Arab and a non-Arab so they have a diminished target audience. If, for example, an unusual number of Arabs had tickets to board a plane to Israel, that would immediately cause reason for suspicion. Israel has methods of dealing with such matters.

But in America, that would be virtually impossible. Airport security agents are only trained to detect dangerous objects such as explosives, guns, knives, etc.; no attention is paid to the personal character of the passengers going through security on their way to boarding a plane.

But let's assume security was trained to recognize Arabs or people of Arab or Middle Eastern origin. To refuse a person a seat on a plane because he or she has an Arab name, looks Arab or is of Arab descent, would violate the civil rights codes of the United States. For all practical purposes, this type of security screening would be impossible to implement.

Lie Detectors

Another possible measure to take to ensure the safety of an aircraft would be to ask the passengers' intentions and use a lie detector to determine whether they were telling the truth: Are you flying from point A to point B? Or are you boarding the plane to do harm? Could a lie detector really determine a passengers' level of nervousness and anxiety? Based on the information available to us this could be done electronically; however, this raises another problem. Many people are extremely nervous when traveling, particularly on airplanes. Some people even take tranquilizers in order to force themselves into the confines of the small cabin of a plane because they are claustrophobic. That, quite possibly, would skew the outcome of a lie detector test. So once again, we see that we are standing before a problem that is not easily solved.

Nevertheless, the Bible tells us, *"...when they shall say, Peace and safety; then sudden destruction cometh upon them..."* (1st Thessalonians 5:3). We may not see how or when the precise fulfillment of this verse will take place, but we do know with absolute certainly that it will be fulfilled.

People all over the world will be safe and secure. But we must add that it's not a lasting peace, because all of man's security is subject to a time limit.

Chapter 7

NOT ARMAGEDDON

The act of terrorism against the United States did not mark the beginning of Armageddon, nor does it have a direct relation to Armageddon. Why not? Because it is located in the wrong geographic area.

The Battle of Armageddon is described in Revelation 16:16 with few words: *"And he gathered them together into a place called in the Hebrew tongue Armageddon."* Geographically this battle is located in Israel, not in the United States. The Hebrew name for Armageddon is "Har Megiddo." Today the center of Megiddo is a historical hill of great significance. This archaeological treasure represents thousands of years of Israeli history. Often this site is called "Tel Meggido," which means "hill." But this hill is man-made and dates back to approximately 2000 B.C. Megiddo is located on the south edge of the plain of Esdraelon. It was here where Deborah defeated Sisera; Barak gained victory over the king of Hazor; and Josiah died.

Therefore, if it's not Israel, then it's not Armageddon— and New York is not Israel.

We must also point out that it is the Lord God Himself

who will gather the nations together at Armageddon. The purpose of that gathering is two-fold:

1) judgment upon the nations

2) salvation for Israel

The prophet Joel speaks about this final battle in chapter 3 verse 2: *"I will also gather all nations, and will bring them down into the valley of Jehoshaphat, and will plead with them there for my people and for my heritage Israel, whom they have scattered among the nations, and parted my land."* Note that "all" nations are involved against the one nation, God's chosen: Israel.

The September 11 terrorist attack was not perpetrated by a nation, but by a well-organized band of terrorists.

Also notice God's reason for the final battle which is called the Battle of Armageddon: The nations of the world have *"…parted my land."* This is extremely significant to us today because in reality, all the nations of the world are parting the Holy Land. No nation on the face of the earth stands with Israel declaring that the Promised Land belongs to the descendants of Abraham, Isaac, Jacob: the Jewish people. All nations without exception have parted the land of Israel. They have given the right of ownership of that land to Lebanon, Syria, Jordan and Egypt. Now the nations all agree to establish a homeland for Arab settlers in Judea, Samaria and Gaza.

In principle the nations agree with the Arabs, who are now called "Palestinians," in that they should be the rightful owners of all of Judea and Samaria, the Gaza Strip and at least half of Jerusalem.

Most of us don't realize the weight of this matter. This

support of the Arabs places each nation and government of the world in direct opposition to the Creator of heaven and earth, the God of Israel.

Not Mystery Babylon

Furthermore, New York is not Babylon either, because this does not fit in the dispensation of time. The Battle of Armageddon has a purpose, as we already mentioned: the judgment of the nations of the world who have unrighteously taken it upon themselves to divide the inheritance God gave specifically to the children of Israel and give it to the Arabs.

But this battle cannot take place until and unless the Church of Jesus Christ is removed from this world. Why? Because the Church is the light of the world. Only when total darkness comes upon the earth can Satan and his cohorts deceive the entire world into believing that peace has now been established. Only through deception can humanity be convinced that they by themselves, under the leadership of Antichrist and the false prophet, have finally achieved security the world over.

The key person in this peace movement will be a man who can bring about compromises as no one else in history.

We don't need to speculate about the future of the United States. The terrorist act of September 11, which took the lives of thousands of innocent civilians unexpectedly, has become a major cause for America to draw closer to the world and the world to draw closer to

America. As you read these lines, many compromises are being made among the nations.

Peaceable Deception

Let us consider Daniel 11:21–24: *"And in his estate shall stand up a vile person, to whom they shall not give the honour of the kingdom: but he shall come in peaceably, and obtain the kingdom by flatteries. And with the arms of a flood shall they be overflown from before him, and shall be broken; yea, also the prince of the covenant. And after the league made with him he shall work deceitfully: for he shall come up, and shall become strong with a small people. He shall enter peaceably even upon the fattest places of the province; and he shall do that which his fathers have not done, nor his fathers' fathers; he shall scatter among them the prey, and spoil, and riches: yea, and he shall forecast his devices against the strong holds, even for a time."* Notice the words *"peaceably," "flatteries"* and *"deceitfully."* This sounds very much like the politicians of our day who do everything in their power to tell potential voters that they alone can solve the problems of the world. But once elected, they do not have to keep any of those promises.

The Antichrist will be so successful that the nations of the world will worship him. Under the inspiration of the Holy Spirit, the apostle Paul writes the following in 2nd Thessalonians 2:4: *"Who opposeth and exalteth himself above all that is called God, or that is worshipped; so that he as God sitteth in the temple of God, shewing himself that he is God."* These words clearly reveal that the Battle of Armageddon can only take place after global peace has been established—and that is not the case today.

Power To The Beast

We have discussed the need for the entire world to unite in order to effectively fight terrorism. The following is an article from the *Financial Times*, September 17, 2001, Page 6:

> EU transport ministers have agreed jointly to urge the 187 member countries of the International Civil Aviation Organization at their general assembly in Montreal from September 25 to step up preventative measures and monitor their implementation.
>
> The EU is especially concerned that some countries have not required domestic flights to meet the tough security standards of international flights. They want annex 17 of the Chicago Convention that sets air safety rules to be changed to cope with the new threats.
>
> At a special weekend meeting, the EU ministers also agreed to review European procedures to ensure uniform application of safety measures. In particular they agreed that "document 30" of the European Council of Civil Aviation be implemented fully to ensure all countries handle passengers and baggage uniformly.
>
> The ministers agreed experts from governments and the Commission should start examining plans for better safety co-ordination and possible EU legislation.

That means Revelation 17:13 must be fulfilled. The people of the world must come to be of "...*one mind*" and we already have seen this, based on the many declarations of world leaders. Things are in the process now.

But this verse says much more: "...*and shall give their power and strength unto the beast.*" This is much more than just agreeing on a united policy; it clearly tells us that the governments of the world will surrender their political authority and military strength to this one genius, the man called the Antichrist, the evil one, the beast posed by the devil.

Life For The Cause

During the terrorist attack, we learned that these terrorists were totally dedicated people. They gave their lives for the cause. This type of behavior is unheard of in modern times. Although on Memorial Day and other national holidays, we hear the statement, "They gave their lives for their country," the sentiment really isn't true. A soldier who fights in a war never gives his life for his country; his life is taken away by the enemy. Soldiers face soldiers; one is killed as the other kills. No one goes out and says, "I am going to die for my country," meaning that he would deliberately give up his life. Instead, every soldier hopes and prays that when all is over, he will return home safely.

These terrorists, however, do not hesitate to give their lives for the cause. That places us against a totally new enemy the majority of the world has never thought about seriously before September 11th.

Coalition Building

During the Gulf Conflict we saw a preview (not the real thing) of the fulfillment, "...and shall give their power and strength...." This was one of the most difficult things to do; uniting the world's armies, including Arabs, against one Arab country, Iraq, where dictator Saddam Hussein ruled. He had invaded, subdued and occupied Kuwait.

President George Bush, the father of our current president, successfully unified virtually the entire world against Saddam Hussein. The United States was in charge and the participating nations had to surrender their "power and strength" to the authority of the U.S.A. This was achieved through a delicate political balancing act.

We all know that it took six long months for a military force to be activated for Desert Storm.

I realize that this may not be the best example because the evil one was definitely Saddam Hussein, and the rest of the world under the leadership of the United States had a legitimate cause to reestablish security for the region and world peace. But this is a shadow of things to come on a much greater scale.

The Last Empire

The prophet Daniel speaks of this last world empire with the final ruler unto whom all the world will gladly surrender its power and strength: *"After this I saw in the night visions, and behold a fourth beast, dreadful and terrible, and strong exceedingly; and it had great iron teeth: it devoured and brake in pieces, and stamped the residue with the feet of it: and it was diverse from all the beasts that were before it; and it had ten horns"* (Daniel 7:7). This is going to be a political system under a leader unprecedented in the history of mankind. Daniel wrote, *"...diverse from all the beasts that were before it...."*

At this time, it is absolutely unthinkable that the United States would surrender its political sovereignty, economic power and military strength to one person. But when we compare the progression of things in these endtimes, we begin to realize that this will happen in the future. That's why we have the prophetic Word. God challenges us, *"Ask me of things to come."* The apostle Peter very clearly and definitely admonishes every believer to heed the prophetic Word: *"We have also a more sure word of prophecy; whereunto ye do well that ye take heed, as unto a light that shineth in a dark place, until the day dawn, and the day star arise in your hearts"* (2nd Peter 1:19). The last book of the Bible offers this promise, *"Blessed is he that readeth, and they that hear the words of this prophecy, and keep those things which are written therein: for the time is at hand"* (Revelation 1:3).

Ultimate Control

Although Israel does things "the old-fashioned way" when it comes to airport security, as we discussed earlier, it is Israel who is developing the most sophisticated electronics in the world. With this in mind, is it possible to build an electronic security system that would reveal even the smallest detail about each passenger who boards a plane? I am convinced that it is. We already have the technology to use computers to measure brain waves. If this can be fully developed, then the true intention of every passenger going through this control system might be exposed.

The news media reported about some of the terrorists who had learned to fly a plane in Florida. They were acting strange and abnormal, but that's not surprising; after all, they had to go to school and learn aviation, knowing all the while that their instruction was to serve only one purpose, their own death and the destruction of thousands of other lives. Such a person cannot be normal and his behavior must be different; surely electronics could be developed to detect such characteristics.

We discussed this subject in detail in our recent book, *The Coming Digital God.* The following is an excerpt from an interview with computer expert Jerry Brown:

Q: The ultimate global society will be controlled by a man-made image. This man-made image must be related to a computer because a computer is today's authority in data control, identification and numerous other important functions. If this image is able to recognize who is worshipping it, we must answer an important question: Is artificial intelligence possible?

A: The answer to that question depends on your definition of "artificial intelligence." If "intelligence" means that a computer can make decisions based on its own input, and base these determinations on its past findings, then the answer is "yes." In other words, if a machine can "learn" from past mistakes, and won't make those mistakes again, some people would classify that as intelligence. That means it's a thinking, targeting thing. Making the leap between that type of intelligence and becoming self-aware by saying, "I know I'm intelligent" is quite a jump and one that I don't see happening in the near future. I'm not sure that in my lifetime a computer will become so intelligent that it considers itself a being and understands what it does.

Q: Are you saying it is impossible after your "lifetime"?

A: I don't believe that anything is impossible anymore after watching everything that has transpired within the last ten years. On the other hand, setting up a computer's learning curve so that it learns by action is happening today and it's happening commercially. Advanced implementation of this logic, called "fuzzy logic" is found in industrial robotics worldwide. I know they're doing it at MIT and Stanford. A certain level of computerized intelligence exists. That's a given. Computers already control the markets. You don't control the markets; I don't control the markets. Not even the stockbrokers control the markets. The markets are actually controlled by the systems in the middle that initiate and consummate the orders. The brokers can initiate orders, but the stock markets themselves had to put in some curbs on computer trading in the past. The computers are following their own programs of stock trends. They are automatically buying and selling large blocks of stock at computer speeds without any human input and that was one major reason why the stock market was knocked back several years ago.

Q: At this point in time, with the exception of sharing information, can one computer learn something from another one? And if so, how?

A: Downloading is the key. When you put a pile of bolts and chips together, you basically have a dumb computer. You download to that computer to make it smart. Think of your desktop computer running the Windows operating system. That was really downloaded from another computer. It may be on a CD when it gets there but it's still logic that was created elsewhere that you put in your computer. It makes your system accurate to a certain degree, so it runs on the same program the other computer is running. Before this process began, your computer was literally dumb; it only had the capability of receiving "knowledge," but after the download of the new software your computer has suddenly become "smart."

60

Q: Does that mean I can continue to implant more knowledge into my computer and outsmart you?

A: I suppose now is the time to talk more specifically about "artificial intelligence." Are machines smart? I don't know about you, but I am constantly corrected by calculators and spell checkers. Does that make the computer smart? No. Can it outsmart me? You bet! Is it smarter than I am? It's not even close. I can download massive amounts of specific "smarts" into my PC. It plays chess much better than I can ever hope to, or rather, it goes through the moves better than I do. But my computer does NOT play. It has no consciousness. I can program my computer to print out the words "I AM CONSCIOUS"; I can even program it to argue that it is conscious, but it is at best a simulation.

Computers "think" by manipulating ones and zeros. But, the ones and zeros by themselves have no meaning. They only have the meaning we attach to them.

Let me explain it another way. The computer knows nothing of what it is doing. It just shuffles ones and zeros. At it's roots, a computer is just a pile of electronic circuits rapidly changing voltage levels. It calculates mathematical problems, but it knows nothing about math.

I am smarter than my son's hamster. My son's hamster is smarter than any computer I have ever worked with. Every computer I have ever worked with can out-perform me in whatever it is programmed to do. But it cannot "outsmart" the hamster. Until the computer can outsmart my son's pet, I will not consider it "artificially intelligent." Perhaps it can only be described as a "simulated thinker."

Q: Are today's computers powerful enough to hold conversations, or to translate from one language to another as you speak?

A: Almost! Today's computing power is smart enough

to do speech recognition, although the software is a little spotty; however, the hardware is easily capable of it. It's all in how the programming is done to make it more accurate. It requires too much of a learning curve by the computer owner to understand your account versus mine. So if your desktop takes your dictation based on your accent, its not going to work when it gets to my side because I speak differently than you do.

The Tower of Babel is being rebuilt. But instead of using bricks and mortar we are using silicon.

In a very short time, you will be able to wake and say, "Computer, tell me the weather in Berlin and send a note to Uncle Helmut wishing him a Happy Birthday in German."

Q: Do you see a computer having the ability to recognize everybody in the world? What needs to be done?

A: You simply have to build its database with the points you want to compare, whether they are fingerprint or retinal patterns. All you have to do is collect the data points and store them in a computer. It can then compare these points much more quickly than any human ever could.

Explosion Of Technology

Everything we write on paper can immediately be considered "old news." The speed of technological development, particularly in the field of electronics, is virtually mind-boggling. What was new yesterday may be outdated tomorrow.

I vividly recall buying our first electronic calculator in 1970. If my memory serves me right, this clumsy, eight-digit calculator cost more than $150. But being a nonprofit missionary organization, we negotiated a discount and on that day Midnight Call Ministry became the proud owner of the electronic "miracle" named Master. Needless to say, it only had four basic functions with a tiny storage capability. Today you can go to a supermarket and buy a watch for $12 that has ten times more functions and hundreds, if not a thousand times more memory.

What's going on in the laboratories of the world's scientists? Few of us want to know, but we can well imagine. I am convinced that the Antichrist will take advantage of the electronic revolution in order to totally control all of humanity. Virtually all technology and inventions give people distinct advantages as well as disadvantages. They can be used for good or evil.

The four planes used in the terrorist attack were designed for good purposes: to transport people from one place to the other quickly and safely. But through the interference of evil man, these machines were used as deadly weapons and became an instrument of death for thousands and a memory of terror to millions, if not billions of people across the world.

Chapter 8

NOT MYSTERY BABYLON

*A*nd the kings of the earth, who have committed *fornication and lived deliciously with her, shall bewail her, and lament for her, when they shall see the smoke of her burning, Standing afar off for the fear of her torment, saying, Alas, alas that great city Babylon, that mighty city! for in one hour is thy judgment come"* (Revelation 18:9–10).

We must reiterate that the horrible catastrophe caused by suicide terrorists is not the Battle of Armageddon, the end of the world, or the judgment of great Babylon. But it is a foreshadow of the things to come, of which the above Scripture speaks.

Our task as believers in the Lord Jesus Christ is to consult Scripture and analyze these events from a biblical perspective. By doing so we will receive information that is not being mentioned by the media. We will begin to understand that events taking place in the United States and elsewhere in the world relate to a global development, leading up the fulfillment of Bible prophecy.

Before we discuss the above Scripture verses and analyze how they forecast their shadows, I would like to use a biblical example to demonstrate the relationship between the prophetic Word and the political geographic world.

In approximately 742 B.C., the prophet Isaiah proclaimed, "...*Behold, a virgin shall conceive, and bear a son, and shall call his name Immanuel*" (Isaiah 7:14). "Immanuel" means "God with us." Isaiah prophesied that God would come to earth in the flesh. This should not have been too difficult for Israel to understand because they had literally and physically experienced supernatural signs and miracles demonstrated by the God of creation. But we all know they did not.

Later, Isaiah the prophet went into detail by actually identifying events or characteristics of the life of the Messiah. Starting in chapter 53, he asked two important questions:

1) *Who has believed our report?*

2) *To whom is the arm of the Lord revealed?*

These questions reveal the people's unbelief thus fulfilling other prophecies that had stated that with seeing eyes they shall not see and with hearing ears they shall not hear.

Who is this man? "*He is despised and rejected of men, a man of sorrows, and acquainted with grief...*" (Isaiah 53:3). That's definitely not what the Israelites wanted for a savior; it went totally against their natural expectations.

Isaiah continued, "*But he was wounded for our transgressions, he was bruised for our iniquities: the chastisement of our peace was upon him; and with his stripes we are healed*" (verse 5). Very plainly, this speaks of someone who would pay for the sin of the people. This prophecy continued: *"He was oppressed, and he was afflicted, yet he opened not his mouth: he is brought as a lamb to the slaughter, and as a sheep before her shearers is dumb, so he openeth not his mouth"* (verse 7). All Bible believers know that this has been fulfilled. Jesus was silent when He appeared before the political and religious authorities in Israel, *"...Jesus yet answered nothing..."* Mark 15:5 confirms.

Even His very character is described, *"...because he had done no violence, neither was any deceit in his mouth"* (verse 9). While on earth, Jesus challenged His enemies, *"Which of you convinceth me of sin?..."* (John 8:46). That's a strong challenge. I'm sure none of us could pose the same challenge because there is sin in our lives. There is much more hidden sin than we may want to admit. It would be extremely embarrassing if our own family, friends and relatives found out the deepest secrets of our lives. This corresponds to the Scripture which says, *"...there is none righteous, no, not one"* (Romans 3:10). *"...all of our righteousness are as filthy rags"* (Isaiah 6:46). But Jesus' character was perfect. That which Adam lost through sin, Jesus demonstrated to the world completely and perfectly.

The prophet was so precise that he tells us that Jesus would not be put to death by Himself, *"...he was numbered with the transgressors"* (verse 12). Two criminals were crucified to His left and to His right.

But there is more. The Bible says, *"...and made intercession for the transgressors"* (verse 12). We remember that Jesus prayed, *"Father forgive them for they know not what they do."* Where was He buried? *"He made his grave with the wicked and with the rich in his death."* He didn't have a plot to His name in which to be buried but He was laid in a rich man's cave which was not His own.

So the Jews had plenty of documentation regarding the coming of the Messiah and His person.

Geographic Reference

The prophet Micah spoke of the place where the Messiah would be born: *"But thou, Bethlehem Ephratah, though thou be little among the thousands of Judah, yet out of thee shall he come forth unto me that is to be ruler in Israel; whose goings forth have been from of old, from the everlasting"* (Micah 5:2).

Daniel gave us the precise time when the Messiah should be born. But when the time came, there was no preparation whatsoever in the religious or political community of Israel. They had the prophetic Word, but they did not heed it.

Moving The World

The birth of Jesus, however, involved the entire known world.

It is fascinating when reading the Scripture that the reports are very accurate; they give details such as the date, place, political rulership, etc. Luke 2 begins with this statement: *"And it came to pass in those days, that there went out a decree from Caesar Augustus, that all the world should be taxed…And all went to be taxed, every one into his own country"* (verses 1,3). This was the first Roman census. All people within the Roman Empire had to return to their place of birth to be registered. Then we read in verse 4, *"And Joseph also went up from Galilee, out of the city of Nazareth, into Judaea, unto the city of David, which is called Bethlehem; (because he was of the house and lineage of David)."*

Now I would like for you to pay careful attention because this clearly demonstrates God's working through good or evil in order to reach His goal; namely, the fulfillment of Bible prophecy.

Where was Mary ready to give birth to her first son? In the city of Nazareth. Well, that's the wrong place. If Jesus was born in the city of Nazareth, then prophecy would be inaccurate. We already read that He was to be born in the city of Bethlehem, which means "the house of bread." Apparently not even Mary or Joseph recognized this important factor mentioned in the prophetic Word. There seems to be no preparation whatsoever for their journey to the town of Bethlehem.

But this did not cause a problem for God. He moved the pagan king, Caesar Augustus, to have all the citizens of his world empire be counted at their place of birth. Thus Jesus was born in Bethlehem, precisely in accordance with the prophetic Word!

I already indicated that the reason for writing this book is to show that God permits the devil to do things in order to fulfill His prophetic Word.

Who Is Mystery Babylon?

Chapter 18 of Revelation deals with a special city called "Mystery Babylon." Who is this Mystery Babylon? Chapter 17 explains who she is. Consider this four-fold criteria by which we may identify the geographic area of Mystery Babylon. This is necessary because some Bible scholars actually believe that New York qualifies for the title of Mystery Babylon — but that's not the case.

1. The blood of the martyrs of Jesus was spilt in that city: *"And I saw the woman drunken with the blood of the saints, and with the blood of the martyrs of Jesus: and when I saw her, I wondered with great admiration"* (Revelation 17:6). This first point is sufficient to prove that Mystery Babylon cannot be New York or any other city except Jerusalem or Rome.

2. The topographical description in the Bible about this city states that it must be built on seven mountains: *"And here is the mind which hath wisdom. The seven heads are seven mountains, on which the woman sitteth"* (verse 9). New York isn't situated on seven mountains; it is built on flat bedrock. Incidentally, this also disqualifies the ancient city of Babel from being rebuilt and becoming the center of the world. However, Jerusalem might qualify since seven hills can be counted if we stretch the borders of Jerusalem a little. Just to be sure that the Bible does speak about the city, the last verse of Revelation 17 makes this crystal clear, *"And the woman which thou sawest is that great city, which reigneth over the kings of the earth."*

3. Revelation 18:3 states: *"For all nations have drunk of the wine of the wrath of her fornication, and the kings of the earth have committed fornication with her, and the merchants of the earth are waxed rich through the abundance of her delicacies."* At this time, Rome is literally and physically not the center of the world. Other cities such as London,

70

Paris, Tokyo and New York certainly seem to be more qualified. But we must not overlook two important items: 1) *"all nations,"* and 2) *"the kings of the earth."* That's about as global as you can get. It does not say "some nations" or "some kings," but very simply, *"all."*

Is there such a city on earth? Our answer is yes, because the entire western civilized world is built on the fundamental principles of Roman law.

The prestigious monthly journal, *National Geographic*, highlighted this fact in its July 1997 issue. Here are some excerpts:

ROMAN ORIGINS

"We know that early on, the Romans were ruled by the Etruscans, a powerful nation of central Italy. Chafing under an often brutal monarchy, the leading families of Rome finally overthrew the Etruscan kings — a revolution that would influence, some 2,200 years later, the thinking of Thomas Jefferson and George Washington.

"In the year 244 AUC (that is, 509 B.C.) the patrician families of Rome set up a quasi-representative form of government, with a pair of ruling consuls elected for a one-year term. This marked the beginning of the Roman Republic, a form of government that would continue until Julius Caesar crossed the Rubicon 460 years later. Those five centuries were marked by increasing prosperity and increasing democracy."

–National Geographic, July 1997, p.15

This early democratic system was barely different than ours today. The article continues:

HOW ABOUT "FAT CAT CONTRIBUTORS?"

"By the second century B.C. the right to vote was so firmly established among the plebeians that Rome developed a vigorous political system-one that would not be unfamiliar to citizens of a modern democracy. There were parties and factions, fat-cat contributors, banners and billboards, negative advertising, and a pundit class to castigate the pols."

–*National Geographic*, July 1997, p.21

Just as a modern democracy, the Romans granted rights, but requested duties.

RIGHTS AND DUTIES OF CITIZENS

"Within the broad sweep of uniformity, Roman administration at the local level was flexible, tolerant, and open.

"When Rome conquered a new province, the defeated general and his army were carted away in chains; almost everyone else came out ahead. The local elite were given positions in the Roman hierarchy. Local businesses gained the benefit of Roman roads, water systems, the laws of commerce and the courts. Roman soldiers guarded the town against pirates and marauders. And within a fairly short period, many of the provincial residents would be made cives Romani — citizens of Rome — with all the commensurate rights and duties."

–*National Geographic*, July 1997, p.30

The Roman Pro-Life movement was actively supported by no one less than Augustus.

ANTI-ABORTION

"Augustus used all the tools of governing. Concerned about a decline in the birthrate, he employed both the stick (a crackdown on abortion) and the carrot (tax incentives for big families). To see if his policies were effective he took a census of his empire now and then.

"Thus it did in fact come to pass in those days that there went out a decree from Caesar Augustus that all the world should be registered. And just as St. Luke's Gospel tells us, this happened 'when Quirinius was governor of Syria,' in A.D. 6."

Under Roman rule, "world citizenship" was real and prosperity greatest.

CITIZEN OF THE WORLD

"History recalls Marcus Aurelius (161B180), the philosopher-king who maintained perspective in the midst of imperial splendor: 'As the Emperor, Rome is my homeland; but as a man, I am a citizen of the world...Asia and Europe are mere dots on the map, the ocean is a drop of water, mighty Mount Athos is a grain of sand in the universe.' Even the cynical Gibbon had to tip his hat: 'If a man were called to fix the period in the history of the world, during which the condition of the human race was most happy and prosperous, he would, without hesitation, name that which elapsed from [A.D. 96 to 180]' — That is, the era of those 'Five Good Emperors.'"

–National Geographic, 7/97, p.35

Without Roman law, today's democracies would not function.

73

LITERACY AND LAW

"The English historian Peter Salway notes that England under Roman rule had a higher rate of literacy than any British government was able to achieve for the next 14 centuries. One of the most important documentary legacies the Romans left behind was the law — the comprehensive body of statute and case law that some scholars consider our greatest inheritance from ancient Rome.

The ideal of written law as a shield — to protect individuals against one another and against the awesome power of the state — was a concept the Romans took from the Greeks. But it was Rome that put this abstract notion into daily practice, and the practice is today honored around the world."

–*National Geographic*, August 1997, p.62B63

Ancient Rome was concerned with citizens' liberty.

INNOCENT UNTIL PROVEN GUILTY

"The emperor Justinian's monumental compilation of the Digests, the Institutes, and the Revised Code, completed in A.D. 534, has served as the foundation of Western law ever since. "Two millennia before the Miranda warnings, the Romans also established safeguards to assure the rights of accused criminals. We can see this process at work in the case against the Christian pioneer St. Paul, as set forth in the New Testament in the Acts of the Apostles.

"In chapter 22 of Acts, Paul is brought before a Roman magistrate on criminal charges — apparently for something like 'provoking a riot.' The police are just about to beat and jail him when Paul pipes up that he is a Roman citizen. That changes everything, and he is

74

permitted to remain free pending a trial.

"Festus responds, in chapter 25, with a lecture on legal rights: 'It is not the Roman custom to hand over any man before he has faced his accusers and has had an opportunity to defend himself against their charges?'"

–*National Geographic*, August 1997, p.68

America's democratic system is clearly modeled after the Roman Republic.

ROME–U.S.A.

"The Roman process of making laws also had a deep influence on the American system. During the era of the Roman Republic (509 to 49 B.C.) lawmaking was a bicameral activity. Legislation was first passed by the comitia, the assembly of the citizens, then approved by the representative of the upper class, the senate, and issued in the name of the senate and the people of Rome. Centuries later, when the American Founding Fathers launched their bold experiment in democratic government, they took republican Rome as their model. Our laws, too, must go through two legislative bodies. The House of Representatives is our assembly of citizens, and, like its counterpart in ancient Rome, the U.S. Senate was originally designed as a chamber for the elite (it was not until the 17th Amendment, in 1913, that ordinary people were allowed to vote for their senators).

Impressed by the checks and balances of the Roman system, the authors of American government also made sure that an official who violated the law could be "impeached," a word we take from the Roman practice of putting wayward magistrates in pedica.

"The reliance on Roman structures at the birth of the United States was reflected in early American popular culture, which delighted in drawing parallels between U.S. leaders and the noble Romans.

"There was a great vogue for marble statues depicting George Washington, Alexander Hamilton, even Andrew Jackson in Roman attire. A larger-than-life statue of Washington in a toga and sandals is still on exhibit at the National Museum of American History in Washington, D.C."

–National Geographic, August 1997, p. 70

It is also of great interest that virtually all leaders of the world subject themselves to the authority of the Roman Catholic pope by requesting an audience with him. Even from the United States of America, an overwhelmingly Protestant country, every president visits the pope after receiving the privilege of an audience with him. That is extremely significant!

4. Revelation 18:10–11,17–18 states: *"Standing afar off for the fear of her torment, saying, Alas, alas that great city Babylon, that mighty city! for in one hour is thy judgment come. And the merchants of the earth shall weep and mourn over her; for no man buyeth their merchandise any more...and all the company in ships, and sailors, and as many as trade by sea, stood afar off. And cried when they saw the smoke of her burning, saying, What city is like unto this great city!"* From a biblical perspective, the sea is the Mediterranean. Israel lies on the Mediterranean coast and John the Revelator was on the Isle of Patmos in the Mediterranean Sea where he received the Revelation and wrote it down.

This further proves that the theory of rebuilding

ancient Babylon is out of the question because smoke from that city would not be visible in the Mediterranean region.

Chapter 9

GLOBAL CAPITALISM

Now let's take another look at the "shadow of Armageddon." The two towers of the World Trade Center symbolized global capitalism even though the designation "World Trade Center" may be exaggerated; after all, the United States represents only 17–18% of the world's economy and the World Trade Center probably represents less than 2%. But there is no greater symbol of capitalism than these two towers that proudly reached into the sky and were visible from miles away. I must admit that the similarity to the events described in Revelation 18 are frightening. The people who stood far off were indeed lamenting the catastrophe that was unfolding before their eyes. Throughout the United States and the world, hundreds of millions of people watched the reduction of these two towers into smoke, dust and ashes within 100 minutes.

What Was The Purpose?

During the days following this horrible tragedy, I heard this question asked many times: "Why did God allow this?" We have already attempted to answer that question, but let's go a little further.

I am fully convinced that the purpose of the attack was not limited to a preview of the Battle of Armageddon. It goes much deeper, and as we will see, it is leading toward the preparation for world unity.

How can world unity emerge through destruction? We need not search any further than recent history, particularly World War II. After the second world war, the European nations sought feverishly to create unity.

Only 12 years after the end of the war in 1957, the Treaty of Rome was signed between six European nations: Belgium, France, Germany, Italy, Luxembourg, Netherlands.

Thus, a total of 220.7 million people became part of a cooperative effort to create a new Europe. After the initial success of establishing the common market, other European countries recognized the promising future of this new movement. A number of nations applied for membership.

THREE MORE NATIONS IN 1973

In January of 1973, three more nations were accepted: Denmark (5.2 million), Ireland (3.5 million) and Britain (57.6 million). Thus another 66.3 million were added! Now united Europe had overtaken the United States in population.

GREECE MAKES NUMBER 10

After 1973, there was an eight-year lull. Then in 1981, Greece (10.3 million) was added to the European Economic Community. This step was rather unusual. Although Greece belongs to Europe, it is more identifiable in association with Mediterranean countries and was expected to be one of the last to be accepted.

When Greece came into the fold of the European Economic Community, the new Europe counted 297 million citizens.

I believe there is a specific reason for having Greece added to Europe in 1981. Earlier, I mentioned that according to the Bible, Greece constituted the third Gentile world empire.

We also saw how the Gentile empires were itemized: Babylon, Medo-Persia, Greece, and Rome, symbolized by four metals — gold, silver, brass, and iron.

Further, we saw that these four empires are identifiable in our day and all four were involved in war in recent decades. The enumeration of these power structures is significant, *"Then was the iron, the clay, the brass, the silver, and the gold, broken to pieces together..."* (Daniel 2:35a). The head, which is Babylon, is not going to be broken first, but the feet, the softest part, the most inferior system. When Daniel interprets the dream, he cautions, *"...it brake in pieces the iron, the brass, the clay, the silver, and the gold..."* (Daniel 2:45). The iron is Rome [European Union] and the brass is Greece.

Therefore, we can expect that Iran [Persia], the silver empire, will one day be added as well. Finally, Iraq, which was ancient Babylon, the gold empire, must be incorporated in the European Union (Roman Empire) as well.

While these conclusions are not clearly visible yet, we know from the Holy Scripture that these empires will become united because they must stand in the final judgment.

1986: EUROPE 336.4 MILLION STRONG
The development of the European Union continued. In 1986, Portugal (9.9 million) and Spain (4.0 million) were also accepted.

81

The EEC in 1986 was thus 336.4 million strong! Less than 30 years after the birth of the Treaty of Rome in 1957, Europe had become the most powerful economic bloc in the world. Since 1994, she has been known as the European Union.

WHO ARE THE TEN KINGS?

It has commonly been believed by many Bible scholars that the European Union was a fulfillment of the resurrected Roman Empire. It was also commonly believed that the E.U. would only consist of ten nations. But as we have just seen, the number rose to twelve when Spain and Portugal were added.

The conclusion that the E.U. would be made up of ten nations originated with a misinterpretation of Revelation 17:12, where it speaks of ten kings.

A VOICE FROM 1967

Midnight Call founder, Dr. Wim Malgo, wrote the following in 1967: "Let us not look for ten countries being members of the European Common Market constituting the fulfillment of Revelation 17:12. Rather we must look for ten power structures that will develop through the European initiative but will be worldwide."

I have always been in full agreement with this statement because the Bible specifically says ten "kings." A king is not a nation, he is an individual person. While it is too early to properly identify what these ten power structures are, there is no doubt that Europe will be number one. This is not only because it has the most educated population, the biggest economic power bloc, and innumerable other advantages, but because Europe is the foundation of our modern civilization and is willing to change.

EUROPE: FIFTEEN NATIONS

On January 1st, 1995, three more nations joined the Union:

Austria (8.0 million), Sweden (8.6 million) and Finland (5.0 million).

At the time of this writing, the E.U. is over 362 million strong. And there more nations, especially from eastern Europe, that are waiting to join. Therefore, we must emphasize that it appears the E.U. will continue to grow in size and number. I believe it will eventually expand across the globe comprising ten power structures.

Most important, however, is to understand that no other group of nations can claim to be the center of the world's intellect except Europe. They are the originators of our global westernized civilization. No doubt, Europe is being readied for world dominion!

–*How Democracy Will Elect the Antichrist*, pages 166, 167, 168, 171

The horrendous destruction due to World War II laid the foundation for creating a new society which is now the richest in the world—and that's only the beginning.

Europe is not a country but a continent of diverse people, languages, culture, tradition and religion: therefore, world unity will be achieved through diversity, just as it was done in ancient Roman times.

In contrast to Europe, America is unified. We have one flag, one president, one language, one law and only two main political parties, which happen to be very similar to each other (the Democrats are trying to be Republicans and the Republicans are trying to be Democrats). Therefore, it is impossible for America to unite the nations of the world. But under the flag of the European Union, it is only natural. By law, each nation is allowed to keep its language, national identity, culture and tradition alive within the Union. It stands to reason that under the

European system, membership is virtually unlimited.

How did this unity come about? Through war.

The United States underwent a similar experience during the Civil War. The diversity between the southern Confederacy and the northern Union was solved through a war. Again, unity was accomplished through war.

War Against Whom?

Particularly during the first few days after the terrorist attack, a lively discussion often centered on President Bush's statement that this was an act of war. But war against whom?

It seems that the power center behind this act of terrorism points to one man, Osama bin Laden, a citizen of Saudi Arabia, member of the royal family. But bin Laden is not a country; he does not have a geographic residence, an army, an economy or a national currency. Apparently, his people operate throughout the world, his financial assets are globally distributed in banks, and his whereabouts are always secret.

This should remind us of Israel who, after having fought five wars against known enemies such as Egypt, Jordan, Syria, Iraq and Lebanon, is fighting a people who are not established as independent nations. The Palestinian Arabs do not have a specific boundary, organized armed forces, (other than an inflated police force), or its own currency. They exist only on the good will of Arab nations and on generous donations by the Europeans, Japanese and Americans.

Israel has very cautiously operated against terrorism

for many years, but in most cases they have been condemned. The United States protested when Israeli forces penetrated the Gaza Strip under Palestinian authority. When Israel killed terrorist leaders before they could inflict damage to Israel, the entire world, including the U.S.A., strongly opposed those actions. National Columnist Cal Thomas wrote for the *Tribune Media Service*:

> Something else died on Tuesday, in addition to thousands of innocent people. It was the doctrine of moral equivalency — the idea that people everywhere are just like us, or can be made so by meeting their demands.
>
> Secretary of State Colin Powell said Wednesday that the United States will go after terrorism wherever it is found. That's a nice change from the State Department's criticism of Israel for doing precisely what we now plan to do. Powell has said that Israel went "too far" when it retaliated against terrorists who killed Israeli civilians. Powell seems to indicate that America's approach to terror will be limitless. If that's good policy for America, why isn't it good policy for Israel?
>
> Perhaps the idea of a "cycle of violence" in the Middle East has also died. That phrase implies that there are no perpetrators and no victims. Funny how U.S. leaders stop talking about such things when Americans bleed and die.
>
> The enemies of religious pluralism, tolerance and other U.S. values see it as their divine mandate to eradicate people who do not believe as they do. These are not people who can be mollified, coddled or persuaded to think and act differently. For them, it is not an aberration to kill what they regard as the enemies of Islam. It is their commission and duty.
>
> Before plotting future approaches to terrorism, it would be well to consider our past approaches, which

clearly failed.

–*The State*, 9/16/01, P.A9

Now the tables have turned. America must show its own citizens and the world that she has the ability to extract terrorists and bring them to justice. According to common sense and the clear statements of political leaders, military members and intelligent experts, that is absolutely impossible without the cooperation of the international community.

I don't think we need much of an imagination to see the global community drift towards a more deeply integrated society which deals with each other not just for economic advantages, but for security reasons as well.

The New United World

It is no coincidence that the United Nations' headquarters are located in New York City, not far from the site of the World Trade Center. The name of the organization — "United Nations" — says it all and should remind us of the verse we discussed: "...*these have one mind.*" To have one mind simply means to agree with one another. To understand the United Nations' purpose, consider the words found in the *New York Almanac 2000*:

> The United Nations officially came into existence on October 24, 1945, when the charter was ratified by China, France, the Soviet Union, the United Kingdom, and the United States and by a majority of the other signatories.

86

WE THE PEOPLES OF THE UNITED NATIONS DETERMINED

- to save succeeding generations from the scourge of war...
- to reaffirm faith in fundamental human rights, in the dignity and worth of the human person, in the equal rights of men and women and of nations large and small...
- to establish conditions under which justice and respect for the obligations arising from treaties and other sources of international law can be maintained...
- to promote social progress and better standards of life in larger freedom.

AND FOR THESE ENDS

- to practice tolerance and live together in peace with one another as good neighbors
- to unite our strength to maintain international peace and security
- to ensure, by the acceptance of principles and the institution of methods, that armed force shall not be used, save in the common interest
- to employ international machinery for the promotion of the economic and social advancement of all peoples.

HAVE RESOLVED TO COMBINE OUR EFFORTS TO ACCOMPLISH THESE AIMS.

Accordingly, our respective Governments, through representatives assembled in the city of San Francisco, who have exhibited their full powers found to be in good and due form, have agreed to the present the Charter of the United Nations and do hereby establish an international organization to be known as the United Nations.

Purposes. The purposes of the United Nations are set forth in Article 1 of the Charter. They are: 1). To maintain international peace and security. 2). To develop friendly relations among nations based on respect for the principle of equal rights and self-determination of peoples. 3). To cooperate in solving international problems of an economic, social, cultural or humanitarian character, and in promoting respect for human rights and fundamental freedoms for all. 4). To be a center for harmonizing the actions of nations in the attainment of these common ends. (page 718).

It is difficult to argue against the noble principles outlined above. We must note again that this was the result of World War II. But how we implement the laws of the United Nations without interfering in internal matters of sovereign nation states is quite a different matter and extremely difficult at that!

After reading these few words, which are an extraction from the full Charter of the United Nations, we notice the words "to ensure...that armed force shall not be used save in the common interest." In other words, no nation has the right to go to war unless the common interest is established (that means authorization by the members of the United Nations.) And we all know that hasn't worked.

The United States has withdrawn its support to a number of principle programs operated by the United Nations. Most interesting is that the United Nations, which condemns nations that are not in cooperation with the fundamental Charter of the United Nations, has condemned Israel more than any other nation although it was the United Nations who put her stamp of approval on the establishment of the nation of Israel in November 1947.

A newsletter dated May 1995 issued by the American

Sovereignty Action Project strongly criticizes the operation of the United Nations:

> "The bombing of the federal building in Oklahoma City was horrible enough without one prominent commentator trying to transform the incident into a demand for the United States to give up its sovereignty. But that is exactly what a senior fellow of the Council on Foreign Relations (CFR), Jessica Mathews, did in a column in the April 24 *Washington Post*. Mathews tried to connect the Oklahoma bombing to the gas attacks in Japan, saying the nations of the world are vulnerable to a 'rising wave of international crime' that is 'a profound challenge to national sovereignty.'
>
> *The Washington Post* reported that the group of radical Muslims accused of plotting the `war of urban terrorism' in the U.S. that included the 1993 World Trade Center bombing had contacts in the U.N. who were prepared `to let them inside with a bomb.'" It was unclear who the intended targets of a bombing inside the U.N. might be.

In general, the American population strongly opposes the yielding of any sovereignty to the United Nations or any other international organization.

In the meantime, the world's composition has changed drastically. Although America experienced an unprecedented boom with high employment, low inflation, the most drastic reduction in crime and an exceptionally strong currency during the 1990's, skeptics all over the world over pointed to the reason of such success: the American worker. Not only were millions of jobs exported to the United States by Europe in particular, but an unprecedented volume of foreign investment flooded into the United States. The U.S. Commerce

Department reported that in 1997 only 69.7 billion dollars were invested by foreigners in the United States: that number had skyrocketed to 320.9 billion in 2000.

In 1996 the American work force replaced Japan as the second hardest-working people in the world and in 1998 it became number one as American workers worked even harder to displace Singapore as the world's number one workforce.

This tendency clearly shows the dependency on globalism and it will undoubtedly continue to increase as large corporations merge into gigantic corporations who have little, if any, interest in the sovereignty of nationals. Global corporations profit wherever, whenever, and however it can be achieved.

Chapter 10

CHURCH AND GOVERNMENT

"*For many deceivers are entered into the world, who confess not that Jesus Christ is come in the flesh. This is a deceiver and an antichrist*" (2nd John 1:7).

The denial that Jesus Christ, the Son of God, came in the flesh is not exclusively a Muslim teaching, but is found in all religions, including Churchianity which denotes a church, denomination, group of people, or individuals who do not believe that God came in the flesh and fulfilled the prophecies of the Old Testament. These are the "antichrist's" that John was describing in his letter. They have reduced the Bible to nothing more than a good book that offers guidelines for morals and is a great contribution to the advancement of civilization!

Therefore, Churchianity is another tool Satan uses to unite the entire world and create peace and prosperity for all people. Satan's ultimate goal is to be worshipped as god, elevating himself in the eyes of those who are deceived.

The Bible clearly proclaims, "*...the Word was made flesh, and dwelt among us, (and we beheld his glory, the glory as of the only begotten of the Father,) full of grace and truth*"

(John 1:14). Who is the Word? John begins his Gospel account in this manner: *"In the beginning was the Word, and the Word was with God, and the Word was God. The same was in the beginning with God. All things were made by him; and without him was not any thing made that was made. In him was life; and the life was the light of men. And the light shineth in darkness; and the darkness comprehended it not"* (John 1:1-5). This is history—past, present and future. The Word was from the beginning, and it was made flesh, testifying to all people that salvation is only obtainable in one way, through Jesus.

What is the meaning of the words, *"…the darkness comprehended it not?"* Every person on the face of the earth who does not believe that Jesus Christ has accomplished perfect salvation on Calvary's cross when He poured out His life in His blood are the ones who, *"…comprehended it not."*

Jesus Himself testified to the following in John 3:36: *"He that believeth on the Son hath everlasting life: and he that believeth not the Son shall not see life; but the wrath of God abideth on him."* With this biblical fact in mind, we must conclude that there are only two groups of people:

1. Those who have the Son and subsequently have everlasting life; and

2. Those who do not believe and therefore will not see eternal life but *"…the wrath of God abideth on him."*

As Christians, there is only one way to analyze the terrible event that took place on September 11 on the East Coast of the United States of America: the Word of God. We can also use these fundamental principles when analyzing all previous, present and future events, conflicts and wars. It is always comes back to the Word of God.

Jesus said that those who are born again are the light of the world. We testify to all people everywhere that Jesus saves and He is coming again. There is no other way to heaven but through the name of Jesus which is clearly confirmed in Acts 4:12: *"Neither is there salvation in any other: for there is none other name under heaven given among men, whereby we must be saved."* But we are not the United States of America, nor are we Saudi Arabia, Afghanistan, Britain or Russia. We are the children of God who are scattered all over the world. No matter where one may travel you will always find yourself confronted with born again believers. There were Christians who worked, or were visiting the World Trade Center. Likewise, there are Christians who live in the country from which the suicide terrorist bombers came. Therefore, as true Christians, we must be very cautious regarding our judgment of any nation because the Bible says that the way we judge others is the way we will be judged.

The Crusaders

It seems natural for us to point out the teachings of violence within the Muslim Koran, which we will do a little later, but let us first understand that Churchianity is equally as guilty of preaching and practicing indiscriminate violence against others.

J. M. Roberts wrote the following in, *A History Of Europe* (Penguin Group, 1996, page 148):

The word "crusade" is used very loosely nowadays to indicate a public display of enthusiastic support for almost any cause, but it was for a long time conveniently applied almost exclusively to the succession of military expeditions from western Christendom to Syria and Palestine in the twelfth and thirteenth centuries, whose aim was to recover the Holy Places of Syria and Palestine from their Islamic rulers. Those taking part were assured, on papal authority, of important spiritual benefits; after death, they would enjoy a remission of the time their souls would spend in purgatory, and if they died on crusade they would achieve the status of martyr. Men so assured — even children, on one occasion — kept the Levant in the forefront of the consciousness of western rulers and the Roman Church for more than two centuries.

The first and most successful was launched in 1096, and had been promoted at the Council of Clermont by the pope's own preaching, of which news soon spread. Encouraged by the miraculous and apt discovery of the lance which pierced Christ's side as he hung on the cross, the crusaders recaptured Jerusalem, where they celebrated the triumph of the Gospel of Peace by an appalling massacre of their prisoners, women and children included.

The Second Crusade (1147–9), in contrast to the first, began with an enthusiastic massacre (of Jews in the Rhineland), but thereafter, though the presence of an emperor and a king of France gave it greater social eclat than its predecessor, it was a disaster.

THE AGE OF THE CRUSADES

The first four crusades were the most important and together with the liquidation of their creation, Outremer, make up what is usually thought of as the Crusading era.

AD 1095 Urban II proclaims the First Crusade at the

Council of Clermont. It culminated in:

1099   The capture of Jerusalem and foundation of the Latin Kingdoms.

1144   The Seljuk Turks capture the (Christian) city of Edessa, whose fall inspires St. Bernard's preaching of a new crusade (1146).

1147–9 *The Second Crusade*, a failure (its only significant outcome was the capture of Lisbon by an English fleet and its transfer to the king of Portugal).

1187   Saladin reconquers Jerusalem for Islam.

1189   Launching of *Third Crusade* which fails to recover Jerusalem.

1192   Saladin allows pilgrims access to the Holy Sepulcher.

1202   *Fourth Crusade*, the last of the major Crusades, which culminates in the capture and sack of Constantinople by the crusaders (1204) and establishment of a 'Latin Empire' there.

1212   The so-called 'Children's Crusade.'

1216   *The Fifth Crusade* captures Damietta in Egypt, soon again lost.

1228–9 The emperor Frederick II (excommunicate) undertakes a 'crusade' and recaptures Jerusalem, crowning himself king.

1239–40 'Crusades' by Theobald of Champagne and Richard of Cornwall.

1244   Jerusalem retaken for Islam.

1248–54 Louis IX of France leads a crusade to Egypt where he is taken prisoner, ransomed, and goes on pilgrimage to Jerusalem.

1270   Louis IX's second crusade, against Tunis, where he died.

1281   Acre, the last Frankish foothold in the Levant, falls to Islam.

There were many other expeditions to which the title

95

of 'crusade' was given, sometimes formally. Some were directed against non-Christians (e.g. Moorish Spain and the Slav peoples), some against heretics (e.g. the Albigenses), some against monarchs who had offended the papacy. There were also further futile expeditions to the Near East. In 1464 Pius II failed to obtain support for what proved to be a last attempt to mount a further crusade to that region.

Numerous other publications document Churchianity's excessive use of brutality, particularly the Crusaders.

Thousands of books on European history document that political Christianity produced only a Churchianity that had no relationship to the true Church of Jesus Christ.

Nevertheless, in the eyes of the rest of the world outside of Churchianity, the distinction is not recognized. From a Muslim point of view, either you are a Muslim or an infidel, subject to forceful conversion.

Less than 150 years ago, a Civil War ravaged our nation. Both sides were religiously active, and each claimed that it was fighting for God and country. Such is the danger when one does not clearly distinguish between the Church of Jesus Christ, which consists exclusively of born again believers, and the political church, which I have coined "Churchianity."

How are we then to act as Christians in the United States, or any other country in the world? We are to be obedient to the Scripture. Romans 13:1–6 makes this point unquestionably clear: *"Let every soul be subject unto the higher powers. For there is no power but of God: the powers that be are ordained of God. Whosoever therefore resisteth the power, resisteth the ordinance of God: and they that resist shall receive to themselves damnation. For rulers are not a terror to good works, but to the evil. Wilt thou then not be afraid of the power? do that which is good, and thou shalt have praise of the same: For he is the minister of God to thee for good. But if thou do that which is evil, be afraid; for he beareth not the sword in vain: for he is the minister of God, a revenger to execute wrath upon him that doeth evil. Wherefore ye must needs be subject, not only for wrath, but also for conscience sake. For this cause pay ye tribute also: for they are God's ministers, attending continually upon this very thing."* Some claim that this only applies if the government is benevolent and established on biblical principles; however, I have not read any documentation supporting this in Scripture.

We are to be subject to "higher power." Luther translates the words "higher power" with the words "prevailing authority." To reinforce these words, the Bible continues, *"...there is no power but of God."* Based on this verse, that is indeed the case, *"...the powers that be are ordained of God."*

We must not forget that the apostles Peter and Paul were subject and obedient to the prevailing government, which was the occupational force of Rome. Even Jesus Himself did not in any way oppose the Roman occupational government. In fact, He publicly endorsed the paying of taxes to the occupiers of His country. I choose to follow in the footsteps of my Lord because He clearly told us that His Kingdom is not of this world. We are not fighting against flesh and blood, but against

97

principalities and demonic powers under the heavens which are working in the children of disobedience. Who are the children of disobedience? All those who do not believe that Jesus is the Savior and the only way to heaven.

Chapter 11

ISLAM IN THE ENDTIMES

We have discussed Christianity as a whole and have documented that our religion has collectively accumulated great guilt by politicizing the religion, subsequently using force to spread Christianity in many places. We have emphasized that such religion has no direct relationship to the Church of Jesus Christ, which consists only of born again believers. Of that Church, Jesus said she is a small flock, sometimes despised and rejected, sometimes persecuted, and occasionly killed for their faith in Jesus. That is happening even today.

When we speak about Islam, we must point out that within that religion, the overwhelming majority of members are peace-loving human beings who have their hands full raising families, providing food and shelter, and if possible, raising their standard of living so that their children and grandchildren will have a better life. But when this religion, or any other for that matter, is politicized, then it becomes an extremely dangerous weapon in the hands of fanatics. That has been demonstrated by the many terrorist attacks that have taken place since the establishment of the state of Israel in

1948. The most horrendous act yet, however, is the diabolically inspired slaughter of thousands through the suicide bombing attack on the World Trade Center and the Pentagon.

If, as Christians, we permit the forces of evil to blatantly condemn all Arab and Muslim nations because of this terrible crime against the United States, then the devil has won a great victory. Therefore, whenever we analyze events, tragedies, conflicts and war, we must first apply the rule Jesus gave us to separate the two groups: *"He that believeth on the Son hath everlasting life: and he that believeth not the Son shall not see life; but the wrath of God abideth on him"* (John 3:36).

What Is Islam?

The Arabic word "Islam" can be translated as "submission." Of course, in this case it means submission to the will of Allah. The religion was founded in the seventh century and emphasizes the oneness of God. Its sacred book is the Koran and the only prophet or messenger of the Muslim god is called Allah; Mohammed.

Under the caption, "history," *Webster's New Universal Encyclopedia* states the following (Barnes & Noble: 1997, page 591):

> **History:** Islam began as a militant and missionary religion, and between 711 and 1492 spread east into India, west over N. Africa, then north across Gibraltar into the Iberian peninsula. During the Middle Ages, Islamic scholars preserved ancient Greco-Roman learning, while the Dark Ages prevailed in Christian Europe. Islam was seen as an enemy of Christianity by

European countries during the Crusades, and Christian states united against a Muslim nation as late as the battle of Lepanto 1571. Driven from Europe, Islam remained established in N. Africa and the Middle East.

Islam is a major force in the Arab world and is a focus for nationalism among the peoples of Soviet Central Asia. It is also a significant factor in Pakistan, Indonesia, Malaysia, and parts of Africa. It is the second largest religion in the UK. Since World War II there has been a resurgence of fundamentalist Islam (often passionately opposed to the ideas of the West) in Iran, Libya, Afghanistan, and elsewhere. In the UK 1987 manifesto, *The Muslim Voice* demanded rights for Muslim views on education (such as single-sex teaching) and on the avoidance of dancing, mixed bathing, and sex education.

Is The Koran Divine?

In the book *The Sources of Islam,* authored by the Rev. W. St. Clair-Tisdall, M.A. and translated by Sir William Muir, K.C.S.I, D.C.L., L.L.D., Ph.D., (Bologna), the author analyzes the writings of the Koran, the Muslim's holy book, comparing and highlighting contradictory statements by which he, and the reader, must conclude that the context of the Koran is based on circumstances experienced by the prophet Mohammed and therefore cannot be considered divine.

As the edifice of Islam has its own established character, and differs from all other religions, it is clear that it is the work of one possessed of the highest gifts and power; and, from the beauty of the composition of the Coran we see that he was singularly wise and eloquent. Moreover, from his life as given in Tradition, and the history of his time, the personality of the Prophet

101

is manifest in the Coran. Thus before his flight to Medina, being a mere ordinary citizen of Mecca, he made no mention in the passages given forth there, of force or war for the extension of the faith.

But, FIRST, after the Hegira, when he had gained the powerful body of the Ansars for his followers, he gave them leave to defend themselves and beat off their opponents. Thus in Surah xxii, 40: *Permission is given to them to fight, because they are persecuted...those who have been turned out of their houses without just cause other than that they say, Our Lord is God; and it is allowed by the Commentaries, that this was the first revelation giving permission to fight.*

SECOND, some time after, when Mahomet had gained victories over his enemies, this simple permission was changed into command, as we find in Surah ii. 212, 214: *War is enjoined you, but it is hateful unto you...They will ask thee concerning the Sacred Month, whether they may war therein. Say, — To war therein is grievous but to obstruct the way of God, and infidelity towards him and the holy masjid, and to drive out his people from thence, is more grievous in the sight of God; and temptation (to idolatry) is more grievous than to kill.* The instruction in this passage being that the Moslems should war against the Coreish even in the Sacred months, because they prevented them from visiting the Kaaba.

THIRD, when in the sixth year of the Hegira, the Prophet had conquered the Beni Coreitza and other tribes, he issued still sterner commands against his adversaries, as we find in Surah v. 37: *The recompense of those who fight against God and his Apostle, and study to act corruptly on the earth, is that they shall be slain or crucified, or have their hands and their feet cut off on the opposite sides (of the body) or be banished from the land. Such shall be their disgrace in this world, and in the next they shall suffer a grievous punishment.* The commentators hold that this terrible command relates to idolaters only, and not to the Jews and Christians.

FOURTH. But towards these also, the attitude of the Prophet towards the end of his life entirely changed; and so we read in the last revealed Surah (i x. 5,29) that after the four Sacred months had passed, they should again commence war, as follows: *And when the Sacred months are ended, kill the idolaters wheresoever ye find them, take them prisoners and besiege them, and lay wait for them in every convenient place. But if they repent, and offer up the appointed Prayers, and pay the legal Alms, then dismiss them freely, for God is gracious and merciful...Fight against those who believe not in God, nor in the last day, nor forbid that which God and his Apostle have forbidden, and profess not the true religion, namely, of those to whom the Scriptures have been given, until they pay tribute by the hand, and be reduced low.*

And so we learn from these successive passages in the Coran, that the great and unchanging Almighty God, step by step, allowed his Divine Law to be altered as the Prophet and his followers gradually gained successive victories by the sword. Not only so, but we see the same liberty of change permitted in respect of certain passages in the Coran to be cancelled by other passages; thus in Surah ii.100:- *We abrogate no verse, or cause it to be left out, but we bring in its place a better, or one like unto it. Ah! dost thou not know that God is over all things almighty?*

Hence so long as Mahomet entertained the hope of bringing together both Jews and Christians, and also the Arab tribes, by the retention of some of their national practices, there seemed to him the possibility of uniting all Arabia in one Grand religion. But when he found this to be impracticable, then it remained for him to either abandon and eventually destroy the two former, or else lose the native Arabs as a whole. The objects and the mind of the Prophet are manifest throughout his prophetic life.

Koran: Key To Terror?

The excerpt from the book *The Sources of Islam,* written in the 1800s, is authentically reproduced with the original spelling of names and places. Missionary Reverend W. St. Clair-Tisdall, who spent his life in Persia, apparently wrote the original in Arabic. It is evident from these few pages that the Muslim religion definitely incorporates violence against non-Muslims. While such is no longer generally practiced throughout the Muslim world, it has been clearly demonstrated, particularly during the last 30 years, that fanatical elements within the Muslim religion take advantage of such writings to justify their diabolical deeds: becoming mass murderers while committing suicide.

Particularly since the founding of the state of Israel, militant Muslims have united into groups under different leaders and systems, the most popular being the PLO led by Yasser Arafat. However, all groups spread throughout the Islamic world are united in their goal to eliminate the state of Israel and establish an Islamic state in its place.

Chapter 12

ISRAEL AND ISLAM

When the state of Israel was proclaimed on May 14, 1948, most international observers, military officials and experts in the field gave Israel little or no chance of survival. One of the reasons was that Israel was made up of the remnant of Jews who survived the Holocaust. A large section of the population came from the communist Soviet Union and a significant number of Jews were displaced from their homes and properties by surrounding Arab nations. In short, they weren't really a nation, but a mixed bunch of people with little unity.

Israel did not have a country to establish a military force; even worse, they did not even have a language for communication. Nevertheless, a miracle did occur. Israel stood its ground against five well-armed and established Arab armies: Syria, Iraq, Jordan, Lebanon and Egypt.

Special counsel to President Truman was Clark Clifford, who argued for the recognition of the new state of Israel while James Forstal, U.S. Secretary of Defense, argued against it: "Clark, you just don't understand this...It's a question of arithmetic. Well, there are 45 million Arabs and 350,000 Jews. And the 45 million Arabs are going to push the 350,000 Jews right into the ocean. That's all there is to it!" (page 35: *Israel, A Nation Is Born*).

The new nation of Israel was founded on its own strength, with only limited help from Czechoslovakia, where they purchased remnant second world war weapons. The Jews stood alone; there was no help from Russia or America. Britain had to think about its Arab allies and France had its hands full with colonial countries. But the war of independence was won and Israel continued to exist.

The next significant war was fought in 1967 when Israel, threatened by Egypt, launched a preemptive strike and crippled the Egyptian Air Force. Subsequently, Israeli Armed Forces were standing at the gates of Cairo and Damascus within six days.

Then in 1973 another war was fought when Egypt and Syria launched a surprise attack upon Israel on Yom Kippur, their most holy day. When the war was over Israel was standing at the gates of Cairo and on their way to Damascus. But then they were forced by the U.S.A. and U.S.S.R. to cease from advancing immediately. During and after each war, it was America who forced Israel to surrender territory they had rightfully conquered. That was one contributing factor to Israel's continuous problems with the Arabs; subsequently, the development of terrorism has now reached the shores of America.

Israel Cause For Mideast Conflict?

Since the time that the Jews returned to the land of Israel, it has been generally stated that the Mideast conflict was due to the Jews coming back to the land of Israel. The Arabs desired to establish an Islamic state on the same territory. Such analysis is short-sighted because we have already clearly shown that the conflict dates back over a thousand years. It's the conflict between Islam, Churchianity, and the Jews. Israel happens to be caught in the middle of it.

But before we go on, let me make one point clear: God is in control of Israel. He is also in control of the Muslims and the rest of the world. No matter what is being planned, who unites with who against whom, the victory is ultimately guaranteed for Israel.

The Muslims have not forgotten the terror the Crusaders brought upon them, nor have they forgotten that they were ruled by Europeans who took advantage of their riches, primarily oil. This was done in a competitive manner between Britain and France. So the Middle East conflict is not exclusively focused on Israel, but it is a conflict of gigantic proportion between Churchianity and Islam, literally encompassing the entire world.

Louis Farrakhan

In 1996, my friend Dr. Moody Adams wrote a fascinating book titled, *The Religion That Is Raping America*. On the back cover of the book, the following quotations are highlighted:

> "Oh Washington, D.C. Oh, government of America, you shall pay well for your evil...There is a God on the scene...He's anxious to destroy you. Rush on to your death."
>
> –Louis Farrakhan

"Our confrontation with America was like a fight against a fortress from outside, and today we found a breach to enter into this fortress and confront it."

–Gadhafi

"God will not give Japan or Europe the honor of ringing down the United States; this is an honor God will bestow upon Muslims."

–Louis Farrakhan

How does Louis Farrakhan conclude that the Muslims will bring down the United States? He bases his beliefs on the interpretation of the Koran, which commands Muslims to fight for the faith in order to Muslimize the entire world.

Muslim Terrorist States

Besides the threat against Israel, terrorist movements originating with Muslim fundamentalists have sprung up all over the world.

The first major violation against established international law and United Nations' regulations occurred in Iran when fundamentalist Muslims tried to overthrow the government of Mohammad Reza Shah Pahlavi. We read the following in the *New York Times Almanac* on page 256:

> Religiously inspired protests resulted in widespread violence in late 1978. A military government was installed by the shah on November 6 with Prime Minister Shahpur Bakhtiar given sweeping powers. The shah went into exile on January 16, 1979. On January 31, Iran's dominant religious leader, Ayatollah Ruhollah Khomeini,

108

returned to Iran from his exile in France. Government forces were routed by Khomeini's supporters, and Bakhtiar's government fell on February 11. In 1979 clashes took place between rival religious factions, between religious parties and secular leftists, and between the urban middle class and the disenfranchised poor. Thousands were arrested and executed by the religious militia forces.

Under President Jimmy Carter's leadership the United States undoubtedly underestimated the power of Iran's religious element. Then came the hostage crisis.

On November 4, 1979, militants seized the U.S. embassy in Tehran and held 62 Americans hostage, provoking a long international crisis. An American military raid in April 1980 failed in an attempt to free the hostages. The hostages were finally freed on January 21, 1981, minutes after Ronald Reagan's inauguration. The following day Iran's president, Abolhassan Bani-Sadr, was dismissed and the Ayatollah Khomeini took over executive power. A new wave of executions followed, with political moderates and non-Islamic religious believers among the principal victims.

The State Department has considered Iran a supporter of terrorism since that time.

Iraq

In the territory of modern Iraq lies Babylon, the ancient capital from where the first Gentile superpower ruled.

The prophet Daniel offers a clear description, not only of the kingdom of Babylon, but also the interpretation of Nebuchadnezzar's dream—of the future of the entire world. Therefore, it is not surprising that Iraq has been in the headlines since the early 1980s.

In 1980, Iraq and Iran were involved in a war that lasted eight years. *The New York Times Almanac* writes:

> On September 22, 1980, a dispute between Iran and Iraq over the Shatt al-Arab waterway flared into open warfare. The war severely crippled Iran. Estimates on casualties range from 450,000 to more than a million dead on both sides, and the war desorbed nearly all Iran's revenue from oil exports, leaving the country nearly bankrupt. The United States was also drawn into the conflict. In 1986, Reagan administration officials attempted to secure the release of hostages in Lebanon by trading arms to the Iranians; and on July 3, 1989, an American ship patrolling in the Persian Gulf accidentally shot down an Iranian civilian airliner, killing all aboard.

The shooting down of a civilian airliner initiated the beginning of the end of that war. In September of 1988, the United Nations brokered a cease-fire but no permanent settlement has been negotiated since that time. In the meantime, Iraq developed into an aggressive militant Muslim nation. The intentions of expanding Iraq's territory which led to the Gulf Conflict, were made public.

> On August 2, 1990, 120,000 Iraqi troops invaded, occupied, and later annexed neighboring Kuwait. The invasion was met with almost universal disapproval, led by the UN Security Council and U.S. troops were deployed to Saudi Arabia to defend it against a possible invasion. Coalition forces eventually totaled 500,000 troops from 13 countries.
>
> After a six-week air war that destroyed most of Iraq's military capabilities and much of the country's infrastructure, Allied ground forced liberated Kuwait and occupied much of southern Iraq in only four days.

To understand the ascension of Saddam Hussein, consider this excerpt from our book, *Saddam's Mystery Babylon*, page 216-220:

HUSSEIN'S ISLAM: FOR PUBLIC CONSUMPTION?

Although not regarded as a religious man, in recent times, Saddam has taken a more public profile in Islam and has called for a "jihad" (holy war) against the Allied forces. His pilgrimage to Mecca and televised scenes showing him lifting hands to "Allah" in prayer have probably been for public consumption rather than expressions of true Islamic faith.

Like many leaders in the West, Hussein might only call on the Divine when things are going hopelessly bad for him in the political or military realm. The phrase ALLAHU AKBAR (God is Great) was added to the Iraqi flag in January, 1991 during the Persian Gulf crisis.

Nevertheless, Saddam appears ready and willing to exploit the religious justification for Islamic "jihad" in the Qur'an, the Muslim holy book which commands that "infidels," (non-believers in Islam) be killed, or at best, be forced into submissive tribute to Islamic overlords.

THE TWO HOUSES OF ISLAM

While it is difficult to measure the degree of actual religious motivation of Saddam Hussein and his true adherence to Muslim religious teaching, there is no doubt whatsoever that he will exploit it whenever possible.

This translates into political policy that has "religious/moral authority" in the Arab world. It is obvious that the teeming Arab masses want an ultra-strong leader who will fearlessly blacken the eye of the West when any perceived Arab/Islamic interest or policy is challenged.

Meanwhile, the sentiment toward Israel, of course, is the desire for total annihilation.

Since these sentiments have Qur'anic and Hadithic religious foundation, they are held with impunity and resolute conviction. Terrorism or outright military destruction are viewed as Allah's perfect and holy will against the "infidel," that is, anyone who is not Muslim.

The religious accommodation in Islam, reserved for Jews and Christians as "people of the Book," is applicable only when those populations are willingly submissive to all Islamic dictates and humbly accept the status of "dhimmitude," paying heavy taxes as well. Any rebellion cancels the accommodation and is to be answered with the sword.

That is fundamental Islamic doctrine. Those of other religious persuasion, such as Hindus, Bahais, Buddhists, or whatever — they are simply to be exterminated when Islam takes over the territory in question. That, too, is fundamental Islamic doctrine. Westerners should understand that within Islam, there is no "separation of church and state." Islam rules in the affairs of Muslims across the entire spectrum of life, from food and clothing to politics and relationships between men and women. Everything.

The "House of Islam," according to Islamic teaching, is divided into two parts: Dar Al Islam and Dar Al Harb.

DAR AL ISLAM/DAR AL HARB

The "domain of the faithful," is "Dar Al Islam." That translates into the territory now occupied and governed under the Islamic religion. In the Muslim religion, once territory is conquered for "Allah," it is considered the eternal property of Islam, and war ("jihad") is always justified — in fact, commanded by the Qur'an — to gain it back.

That alone is one simple reason why Israel will never

be granted "peace" by the Islamic hordes that surround her. She will only be granted peace through the miraculous intervention of the Antichrist, who will somehow temporarily tame the Islamic religious sentiment to destroy Israel.

In contrast to "Dar Al Islam," all other real estate on the globe is referred to as "Dar Al Harb," the "domain of those whom Islam is at war with until judgment day," which is the remainder of the world in which Islam is not the dominant religious and political philosophy. Thus, the ultimate goal of religious Islam, at least on paper, is the subjugation of the entire world, by the sword if necessary.

Most Western people have no idea that this is a central Muslim doctrine. But it cannot be passed off as the fuming of just a couple of wild-eyed fundamentalist mullahs.

THE FATHER OF MODERN-DAY TERRORISM

The unquestioned spiritual father of modern-day fundamental Islam (and modern-day terrorism) is the now-dead Iranian Ayatollah Ruhollah Khomeini. Here's how Islam's leading spiritual authority put it:

"The governments of the world should know that Islam cannot be defeated. Islam will be victorious in all the countries of the world, and Islam and the teachings of the Qur'an will prevail all over the world."

Fundamental Muslims believe this to be their bone marrow and teach it. I will never forget watching the television coverage of Khomeini's funeral. Huge masses of people appeared to be almost going out of their minds with grief and emotion.

So revered was Khomeini that the hysterical mob dumped his body out on the ground and ripped away pieces of the dead man and his clothes, simply to get a part of the man they believed would lead them to a global Islamic resurgence.

113

THE ACTUAL WORDS OF THE "PROPHET" MOHAMMED

Should you still be unsure about Islamic doctrine in this matter of reconquering territory formerly occupied and controlled by Islam, and expanding into formerly non-Islamic countries, let's look at the actual words of Muhammed:

"Regarding offensive wars or imposing the Islamic religion on people by war, Muhammed said: 'I was commanded to fight people until they say, 'There is no God but the only God, and Muhammed is the apostle of God,' and they perform all the Islamic ordinances and rituals."

"We also examined Muhammed's attitude toward the apostate: He made it clear that the apostate must be sentenced to death. He said about those who relinquish Islam: 'Whoever changes his faith...kill him!'"

Libya

Libya was ruled by a monarchy until 1969. Due to the discovery of significant reserves of oil, the country was transformed from one of the poorest states in Africa to one of the wealthiest.

Then on September 1, 1996, Colonel Muammar al-Qaddafi rebelled against the monarchy and through a military coup he established the Libyan Arab Republic. Qaddafi was quickly to expel all foreign troops, close foreign libraries and cultural centers. Foreign assets were nationalized. Muammar al-Qaddafi became the absolute dictator of Libya.

Relations between Libya and the United States were very hostile in the 1980s. On May 6, 1981, the United States closed the Libyan "People's Bureau" (embassy) in

Washington, D.C. On August 2, 1981, American jets shot down two attacking Libyan warplanes as U.S. naval forces conducted exercises in the Gulf of Sidra, which Libya claims as national waters. In 1986 the United States imposed economic sanctions on Libya, ordered Americans to leave the country, and froze Libyan assets in the United States. Another clash in March 1986 ended with the loss of two Libyan ships.

On April 5, 1986, Libyan-sponsored terrorists bombed a nightclub in West Berlin, killing two U.S. soldiers; in response, American bombers attacked Tripoli and Benghazi on April 14 in an apparent attempt to kill Co. Qaddafi himself. In 1990, investigators announced they had linked Libyan agents to the bombing of a Pan Am Jet over Lockerbie, Scotland, in 1988.

Elaborate diplomatic maneuvers in 1998 and 1999 led finally in April to President Qaddafi handing over two Libyans for trial in the 1988 bombing of Pan Am flight 103. U.N. sanctions were thereby automatically suspended but the U.S. announced that its anti-terrorism sanctions would continue. In late April, the U.S. eased food and medicine sanctions.

–New York Times Almanac, P.620-621

Although not all Arab nations oppose the United States, all are unified when it comes to condemning Israel. Nevertheless, no Arab state can be named as a real friend on the level of allies. The only reliable democracy in all of the Middle East is Israel.

Chapter 13

RELIGIOUS GLOBALISM

With the destruction of the World Trade Center, the world's symbol of capitalism and the Pentagon, the strongest military power in the world, virtually all stock exchanges all over the world took a nosedive. These few observations prove the credibility of the prophetic Word beyond a shadow of doubt, which clearly states that the world will be one, it will be of one mind. Today we are seeing the beginning of this and in the near future Revelation 13:3–4 will be fulfilled: *"...and all the world wondered after the beast. And they worshipped the dragon which gave power unto the beast: and they worshipped the beast, saying, Who is like unto the beast? who is able to make war with him?"*

When it comes to interpreting Bible prophecy, there are different opinions, particularly concerning the book of Revelation. However, one point upon which we all agree is that the Bible is the absolute truth and our interpretation is subject to change. So what does the Bible say that need not be interpreted? The words we have just read; namely, that all the world will be amazed about this political genius who will have received authority from the dragon. The people of the world will actually worship the dragon because he will have given his authority to the Antichrist. As a result, they will also worship the beast and loudly proclaim his incomparability and his military invincibility. We all know that is going to happen; it's a biblical fact. It will not be changed because it is the Word of God. The question is: How will it happen? That, of course, is open for interpretation.

One thing is clear: the terrible tragedy of September 11 has brought the world more closely together than ever before. Religious leaders from all denominations and religions took time off and united in prayer to each respective god, asking for courage, strength, wisdom, patience, and protection for those who lost their lives, their families and nation. This was previously unthinkable. The Ecumenical Movement has diligently worked to unite Christianity into one solid voice and has tried to enlist the friendship of other religions for over fifty years. The majority of Bible-believing Christians have publicly protested and warned that such a unity movement is contrary to the Scripture.

During the memorial service for the dead the Friday following the terrorist act, no noteworthy protests were heard or seen throughout the entire American population. A large majority of the world listened solemnly and even participated in the ecumenical religious ceremony in remembrance of the dead.

Successful movements during the last few years have accomplished remarkable progress toward the cooperation between Protestants and Catholics in the

United States. While voices of opposition are being heard, the trend toward the future is definitely unity at any and all costs.

Religion is not taken seriously in Europe anymore, and the ecumenical spirit has progressed much further.

Several years ago when a local mosque in a German city was dedicated, all the churches in the area — Protestants, Catholics and Evangelicals — sent blessings and best wishes for the dedication. As a token of recognition, they pooled their finances and presented the mosque with a beautiful chandelier as a memory of friendship. I am not condemning this action; I am only pointing out that religions are coming together, even Islam and Christianity, which have fought each other bitterly for over a thousand years.

During the progress toward world unity, religion has lagged behind. We have already mentioned that democracy is the leading political philosophy for the world. It originated in Greece, was tested and practiced for a short time in Rome, and from there, spread to Europe and the new world.

We must now soberly ask, "Is it possible to exist and be successful within the family of nations without becoming subject to world democracy?" I dare say no. North Vietnam and Cuba showed the entire world that you do not have a chance to progress and become competitive once you are outside the family of democratic nations.

We saw the practice run or foreshadow of things to come in the Gulf War when the majority of the nations of the world united under the banner of the United Nations and the leadership of the United States to fight one enemy, Saddam Hussein and his army.

We need not belabor the fact that we are already living in a global economy. One only needs to watch the stock exchange to realize how interconnected all the economies of the world are. If the stocks fall sharply in the Far East it affects the stock exchange in Europe and, subsequently, eight hours later, it impacts the United States. As soon as there is a significant rise at the stock exchange in the United States, it immediately affects the stock exchange in Asia some twelve hours later. And so the circle continues.

Look at the international global corporations; virtually none is independent, they are all interconnected.

Financially, we have a world currency for all practical purposes if we consider the fact that any major credit or debit card is considered valid in any country in the world. Whether your currency is the U.S. dollar, the Japanese yen or the British pound, you can go anywhere in the world and make a purchase with your card with the assurance that the transaction is secure and regulated internationally by trustworthy organizations.

January 1, 2002 is the date twelve nations in Europe plan to use the new currency called euro. More will be added as time goes by.

But one problem still exists and that is religion. The brutal, murderous attacks of the suicide bombers was motivated by religion. These poor souls were made to believe that if they surrendered their lives for the cause which they had been brainwashed to believe in, they would instantly be transferred into heaven, becoming the beneficiaries of indescribable glory. This is not too far-fetched when we consider that the Crusaders also believed they would immediately be transferred to heaven if they died in the physical battle against Muslims and Jews when they conquered the Holy Land.

CONCLUSION

"...I am jealous for Jerusalem and for Zion with a great jealousy. And I am very sore displeased with the heathen that are at ease: for I was but a little displeased, and they helped forward the affliction" (Zechariah 1:14–15).

We have seen throughout the pages of this book that the center of controversy is not limited to the terrorist attack on America, but revolves around the Middle Eastern country called Israel. For decades now, Israel has had to deal with suicide terrorists on a daily basis. They are on alert 24 hours a day, 7 days a week. Now that this type of terrorism has reached the shores of the United States, we will become increasingly involved in the debates, cooperation and information-sharing with all other nations around the world.

The message is clear to those who are believers in the Lord: we are entering the final stages of the endtimes which will climax with the Rapture of the Church, followed by the beginning of the Great Tribulation. At the end of those seven years, Jesus Christ will physically return to the Mount of Olives which will result in Israel's salvation and judgment for the entire world.

Because prophecy is the truth of God's Word, it is my prayer that the unbeliever, who may happen to be reading this book, will read the Bible because it is God's message to man.

The Bible's Message

The Bible contains the following prophecy regarding unbelievers: *"For when they shall say, Peace and safety; then sudden destruction cometh upon them, as travail upon a woman with child; and they shall not escape"* (1st Thessalonians 5:3). This verse is very clear: peace and safety will be established on a global basis. It makes no difference whether terrorism is abolished and peace takes its place because it will only be temporary.

The Bible says this regarding those who are children of God: *"But ye, brethren, are not in darkness, that that day should overtake you as a thief. Ye are all the children of light, and the children of the day: we are not of the night, nor of darkness. Therefore let us not sleep, as do others; but let us watch and be sober"* (verses 4-6). We have been warned to be alert. We must not fall into the traps Satan has prepared through the events taking place in this world. We must analyze Satan's work of darkness, recognize the deception and outrightly reject that which is not true.

The Coming Global Prosperity

"For all nations have drunk of the wine of the wrath of her fornication, and the kings of the earth have committed fornication with her, and the merchants of the earth are waxed rich through the abundance of her delicacies"

124

(Revelation 18:3). Notice that this verse is referring to *"all nations"*: all political leaders, or *"kings of the earth"* and all the capitalists, or *"merchants of the earth."*

We need not reiterate that this terrorist act has brought the world closer together politically, militarily and economically. Why? Because all have one enemy: terrorism. From now on, each nation will have to carefully scrutinize all security agreements and make sure they are are being kept by every nation they fly to or have commercial dealings with. No nation will be exempt.

The Beast: The Endtime Hero?

"...and all the world wondered after the beast. And they worshipped the dragon which gave power unto the beast: and they worshipped the beast, saying, Who is like unto the beast? who is able to make war with him?" (Revelation 13:3–4). Notice again that this includes all the world. Apparently the people of the world are overwhelmed by the greatness and success of the one called "the beast." This man will possess a personality of unprecedented qualities.

Finally, there will be religious unity. Members of all religions will be involved in devil worship; *"...they worship the dragon."* These words indicate that they will know that the power and success of the endtime system, under the Antichrist's leadership originates with the devil himself.

Furthermore it says, *"...they worshipped the beast."* This is unusual because worship is reserved for a deity; however, but this person, who is totally possessed by the dragon, will receive worship.

The uniqueness of this personality is mindboggling when we consider the words, *"Who is like unto the beast?"* People all over the world will forget their respective religion because this man will supersede everything: he is number one, a legend in his own time. So the world will pose a challenge to come up with someone who is equal to the beast.

Militarily, he will have complete global rulership. Again, the question is asked, *"Who is able to make war with him?"* Based on this statement, we may expect increasing cooperation between the nations on a military level. The Gulf War was a foreshadow of things to come. The majority of the world's nations either actively or financially participated in the undertaking to rescue Kuwait, a semi-dictatorial nation from Saddam Hussein, the invading dictator of Iraq. The more the nations unite and become stronger, the more the question is valid, *"Who is able to make war with him?"* which can be categorically answered with absolutely no one!

Worshipping the Beast and the Image

"And all that dwell upon the earth shall worship him...And he had power to give life unto the image of the beast, that the image of the beast should both speak, and cause that as many as would not worship the image of the beast should be killed" (Revelation 13:8,15). The word "worship" is the key. Not only will all of mankind worship the dragon, identified in chapter 12:9 as *"...the great dragon...that old serpent, called the Devil, and Satan...."* The beast who receives the power from Satan is also

worshipped and now it goes one step further by demanding that the image be worshipped as well.

There's more. Not only is political, military and religious unity in the making, but verses 16 and 17 say: *"And he causeth all, both small and great, rich and poor, free and bond, to receive a mark in their right hand, or in their foreheads: And that no man might buy or sell, save he that had the mark, or the name of the beast, or the number of his name."* This system will contribute to the world's prosperity as never before in history. Finally, crime will be eliminated; however, there is a price to pay. This price will be the mark of the beast, a subject I deal with in my latest book, *The Coming Digital God.*

The terrorist act against the United States will contribute toward the development I have outlined in this book. When reading your morning newspaper or watching the news, keep the prophetic Scripture in mind which tells us that all the world will worship and honor the beast, and all that dwell upon the earth will rejoice in the glorious global system. But keep in mind that it will all end in immeasurable catastrophe.

Make your decision today and anchor your faith in Jesus Christ, the Son of God who poured out His life in His blood on Calvary's cross and paid for your sins in full.

There is no in-between. You can only belong to one camp or the other. The Bible says: *"He that believeth on the Son hath everlasting life: and he that believeth not the Son shall not see life; but the wrath of God abideth on him"* (John 3:36).

127

▐▐▐➤ *Tap into the Bible analysis of top prophecy authorities...*

Midnight Call is a hard-hitting Bible-based magazine loaded with news, commentary, special features, and teaching, illustrated with explosive color pictures and graphics. Join hundreds of thousands of readers in 140 countries who enjoy this magazine regularly!

▐▐▐➤ *The world's leading prophetic Bible magazine*

▐▐▐➤ *Covering international topics with detailed commentary*

▐▐▐➤ *Bold, uncompromising Biblical stands on issues*

▐▐▐➤ *Pro-family, Pro-life, Pro-Bible*

12 issues/1 yr. $28.95
24 issues/2 yr. $45

Mail with payment to: Midnight Call • P.O. Box 280008 • Columbia, SC 29228   1050

❑ YES! I would like to subscribe to Midnight Call magazine!
   ❑ 12 issues/1 yr. $28.95   ❑ 24 issues/2 yr. $45
   ❑ Cash   ❑ Check   ❑ Master/Visa/Discover
   With Credit Card, you may also dial toll-free, 1–800–845–2420

Card#_____ Exp:_____

Name:_____

Address:_____

City:_____ St:_____ Zip:_____